THE  GIVING TABLE
experience

A guided journey of feasting through Scripture

SALLY CLARKSON
with Joel and Joy Clarkson

TYNDALE
MOMENTUM™

*The nonfiction imprint of
Tyndale House Publishers, Inc.*

Visit Tyndale online at www.tyndale.com.

Visit Tyndale Momentum online at www.tyndalemomentum.com.

Visit Sally Clarkson at www.sallyclarkson.com, www.momheart.org, and www.wholeheart.org.

Visit Joel Clarkson at www.joelclarkson.com.

Visit Joy Clarkson at joynessthebrave.wordpress.com.

TYNDALE, *Tyndale Momentum*, and Tyndale's quill logo are registered trademarks of Tyndale House Publishers, Inc. The Tyndale Momentum logo is a trademark of Tyndale House Publishers, Inc. Tyndale Momentum is the nonfiction imprint of Tyndale House Publishers, Inc., Carol Stream, Illinois.

The Lifegiving Table Experience: A Guided Journey of Feasting through Scripture

Designed by Mark Anthony Lane II

Edited by Anne Christian Buchanan

Unless otherwise indicated, all Scripture quotations are taken from the *Holy Bible*, New Living Translation, copyright © 1996, 2004, 2015 by Tyndale House Foundation. (Some quotations may be from the 2007 edition of the NLT.) Used by permission of Tyndale House Publishers, Inc., Carol Stream, Illinois 60188. All rights reserved.

Scripture quotations marked ESV are taken from *The Holy Bible*, English Standard Version® (ESV®), copyright © 2001 by Crossway, a publishing ministry of Good News Publishers. Used by permission. All rights reserved.

Scripture quotations marked NASB are taken from the New American Standard Bible,® copyright © 1960, 1962, 1963, 1968, 1971, 1972, 1973, 1975, 1977, 1995 by The Lockman Foundation. Used by permission.

Scripture quotations marked NIV are taken from the Holy Bible, *New International Version*,® *NIV.*® Copyright © 1973, 1978, 1984, 2011 by Biblica, Inc.® Used by permission. All rights reserved worldwide.

For information about special discounts for bulk purchases, please contact Tyndale House Publishers at csresponse@tyndale.com, or call 1-800-323-9400.

Library of Congress Cataloging-in-Publication Data
Names: Clarkson, Sally, author. | Clarkson, Sally Lifegiving table.
Title: The lifegiving table experience : a guided journey of feasting through
   scripture / Sally Clarkson, with Joel and Joy Clarkson.
Description: Carol Stream, Illinois : Tyndale House Publishers, Inc., 2017. |
   Companion to author's The lifegiving table. | Includes bibliographical references.
Identifiers: LCCN 2017025536 | ISBN 9781496425232 (sc)
Subjects: LCSH: Dinners and dining—Religious
   aspects—Christianity—Textbooks.
Classification: LCC BR115.N87 C633 2017 | DDC 248.4/6—dc23 LC record available
   at https://lccn.loc.gov/2017025536

Printed in the United States of America

23	22	21	20	19	18	17
7	6	5	4	3	2	1

Contents

To Jesus,
who showed us through so many stories
how important feasting and engaging in ideas over
a meal is to real life. Your example inspires us.

Welcome to the Feast!

He satisfies the thirsty
and fills the hungry with good things.

PSALM 107:9

In all the years that the Clarksons have been a family, feasting together has been a lifegiving activity for us. And we've always *called* it feasting, whether it involves a full-blown banquet, a one-on-one treat of milk and cookies, or a bowl of fresh-popped popcorn around the fire. The word reminds us of God's bounty, the gift of our relationships, and the response of pleasure and thanksgiving that the act of sharing a meal requires of us.

It's no accident that many of our formative and memorable moments over the years have occurred around our various family tables. When my husband, Clay, and I started our family, we were determined to use the family table not only as a source of nourishment, but as a discipling tool and a place to strengthen our bonds of love and belonging. Over the years, as we enjoyed (mostly) healthy, delicious, and sat-isfying food, we also thrived on lifegiving conversation and a steady diet of Scripture shared around the table.

Such scriptural nourishment is at the heart of this guided study. It is intended as a companion to *The Lifegiving Table*, a book I wrote about how feasting together shaped our fam-ily and our shared mission. So rather than focusing on our own story here, we invite you to join us in the experience of feasting on the Word and exploring the scriptural impact of the lifegiving table.

The twelve chapters explore different aspects of food, drink, and celebration in both our physical and our spiritual lives. In each you'll find

- *A pertinent passage (or passages) from Scripture.* We encourage you to feast on it first, savoring it slowly, before moving on.
- *Setting the Table—an imaginative retelling of the passage and a meditation on its meaning.* We've written each of these in a way we hope will make you feel as if you are stepping into the pages of Scripture and experiencing the scenes firsthand. Please keep in mind that we are storytellers and not formal theologians. So any imaginative elements in these stories are not meant to be a statement of how each story *actually* unfolded, but rather our notion of how it *might* have played out. Though we have attempted to be painstakingly attentive to the accuracy of Scripture, we have also

carefully and respectfully used imagery and dialogue that aren't explicitly stated in Scripture. While we hope you enjoy our take on these passages, we encourage you to go back for second helpings to get familiar with the source material yourself and learn the stories straight from Scripture.

- *Table Talk—Conversation Starters.* These are brief questions designed to break the ice in a group study and stimulate both personal reflection and lively discussion.

- *Table Talk—Digging Deeper.* These sections point you toward related Scripture passages and additional questions meant to offer a broader perspective and help you consider the theme of the chapter in greater depth. We've left space in this section for you to jot down your thoughts and ideas, but you can use a separate notebook or journal if you prefer. This section is appropriate for discussion in the group or for individuals to complete later.

There are many possible ways to use this book. While originally envisioned as a twelve-week small-group study, it also will work well for individuals or couples. To enrich the experience, we recommend sharing it over a meal!

As you take this guided journey along with us, we hope you'll take advantage of this opportunity to "hear . . . , mark, learn, and inwardly digest"[1] the nourishing words of Scripture God has provided for us and to truly "taste and see that the LORD is good" (Psalm 34:8). We pray that you will find both strength and sustenance as you explore what it means to feast at the Lord's Lifegiving Table.

Bon appétit!

Sally Clarkson

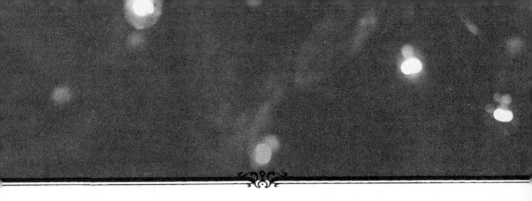

PART I

God Prepares a Table for Us

CHAPTER I

JESUS HIMSELF IS OUR FEAST

As they were eating, Jesus took some bread and blessed it. Then
he broke it in pieces and gave it to the disciples, saying, "Take it,
for this is my body."

And he took a cup of wine and gave thanks to God for it. He
gave it to them, and they all drank from it. And he said to them,
"This is my blood, which confirms the covenant between God and
his people. It is poured out as a sacrifice for many. I tell you the
truth, I will not drink wine again until the day I drink it new
in the Kingdom of God."

MARK 14:22-25

Setting the Table

It was dusk. A subdued quiet had begun to settle over Jerusalem with the impending arrival of the Passover. But in their private room, the evening had begun with festivities. The disciples were exuberant and animated, reflecting on the happenings of the week.

When they entered Jerusalem, Jesus had been hailed as a

coming hero. Some had even called Him a king—a politically loaded word in Roman-occupied Judea if there ever was one. The hint of rebellion and its resulting punishment might have struck fear in their hearts if not for the ecstasy of that moment—the people, waving branches and smiling, looking up in admiration at the little entourage, calling out to Jesus with words of exaltation. It had been too thrilling to let the fear of what might be ruin the enjoyment of the moment.

Now it was Passover, and in the convergence of that holy Jewish feast with their moment of triumph, their hearts rose in celebration for God's faithfulness to them, faithfulness that they were seeing manifest in their lives day by day.

Only those few with a keen eye could see that the Master seemed removed from the festivities, preoccupied and distant. Philip and Andrew saw it. They had been there with that group of Greek scholars when Jesus suddenly began to speak of death, of a grain falling into the ground and dying. It had seemed odd, out of place with the excitement of the moment. People were praising His name in the streets, but He was talking about being "lifted up"—an unsettling phrase tinged with ominous undertones. Now, as everyone jostled around and chatted about the common gossip in Jerusalem, Jesus had stepped into a different room. It seemed odd that He wasn't sharing in their happiness, given His usual spirited participation in their meals together. But the disciples quickly forgot about this and became caught up in conversation. As soon as Jesus returned, the mood of the room began to change. He had stripped away His outer garments and was dressed in the garb of a lowly servant. He carried a basin of water, which He placed at the feet of Bartholomew, and a towel. A hush settled over the gathered group, with only surprised whispers shared between several of the men present.

Was the Master really going to stoop to washing their feet, an action appropriate only for the most humble of household servants? It seemed completely out of place for a man so highly favored. It didn't make sense, but then much of what the Master did was confusing. Perhaps this was just one of His eccentric ways of teaching them one of His truths about the Kingdom of Heaven. So one by one they submitted to this puzzling ritual. Only Peter objected, and Jesus' response to Peter stole away any sense in the group that the evening would be a normal Passover celebration. "Unless I wash you, you won't belong to Me."

Something significant was happening; they could all feel it in the air. When the Master spoke in such a tone, everyone listened closely. As they waited to see what would happen next, Jesus' troubling words from the previous days began to seep back into their consciousness. *You will not always have Me. . . . Unless a kernel of wheat is planted in the soil and dies. . . .* Then He spoke again, and His words cut them like a knife: "One of you will betray Me!"

Betrayal? Who would even think of such a thing? Incredulity and fear began to weave through the threads of their thought. Surely no one would ever give up the Master. He was their Lord. He had brought them life. And yet now

Jesus had all but accused Judas, and Judas, for his part, was slinking away from the group.

Now the fear truly set in. Mere moments before, they had enjoyed the leisure of one another's company, basking in the excitement of the week. Now nothing seemed sure. No one had thought that highly of Judas anyway, but to betray the Master—anything might happen now. A shadow of worry gathered over the group, and they ate in silence.

It was Jesus who broke the quiet. He started to pray, holding up the unleavened bread for the Passover meal. And when He finished His blessing, He began to pass the bread around. "Take it," He said, "for this is My body."

The disciples were simple men, by and large—not respected scholars or leaders in the synagogue. But like all faithful Jews, they understood the significance of the Passover bread. They knew it represented God's provision for their ancestors as they fled Egypt, nourishment for their most basic needs. And now Jesus was associating Himself with that holy symbol. They knew Jesus was sent from God, but this was radically beyond anything they could have imagined.

They had little time to consider this revolutionary notion; Jesus was now blessing the wine. "This is My blood, which confirms the covenant between God and His people."

All of them could sense in their hearts that this was no normal Passover feast. Something larger was at work. In time, the disciples would come to understand that the story of their redemption as Jews was being woven into a larger story, one of a King who had come to suffer and, through that suffering, to triumph over the darkness of the world. And yet, in that early moment, the scope of that story was still unclear to the disciples. They couldn't see the bigger picture and were fearful in that unknowing.

Still, they partook of Jesus' meal. They ate and drank as He asked them. And somehow, in the eating of that bread and the drinking of that wine, a new peace came into their hearts, a peace that transcended understanding. A peace that soothed their anxious spirits the way the bread and wine soothed their hungry bellies.

A peace that somehow contained the redemption of the whole world.

Today, just as in Jesus' time, the world around us feels uncertain, full of danger and sorrow. Like the disciples, who would soon witness Jesus' crucifixion and burial, we will also almost certainly face trouble in the course of our lives. The ground beneath our feet seems to be constantly changing, at one moment firm as rock and at another rolling like waves in a storm. What Jesus longed for His disciples to comprehend, just as He longs for us to understand today, is that when everything around us changes, He is our hope and help. He gives His very self, body and soul, for us. It is He who sustains us and brings us peace.

Jesus wants us to hear the same words that His disciples heard that fateful night so long ago: "In this world you will have trouble. But take heart! I have overcome the world" (John 16:33, NIV). Everything may fall apart around us, but we have a God who has stepped into our time and space, shared our sorrows, and taken them on to Himself. He has made Himself the provision we need in our most difficult moments, not sending down rays of hope from faraway heaven, but walking with us in our suffering.

When we are starved for hope, Jesus gives Himself as our meal. And when we eat of that bread, nothing can remove from us the peace and satisfaction we find there.

Table Talk

Conversation Starters

1. Why do you think it was important for Jesus to personally serve His disciples by washing their feet before the meal?

2. What does it mean to you that Jesus offered His peace to the disciples in the context of a meal?

3. Think of a time when you felt starved of hope. How did that situation resolve (if it did)? What else—besides peace—have you been hungry for?

4. What practical steps can you take to invite God's peace into your own mealtimes—and the rest of your lives?

Digging Deeper

1. *"I am leaving you with a gift—peace of mind and heart. And the peace I give is a gift the world cannot give. So don't be troubled or afraid"* (John 14:27).

a. What is the peace that the world gives—and how is Jesus' peace different? What kind of peace can the world not provide? Write down three different ways in which God's peace transcends worldly peace.

b. If Jesus' peace is something the world cannot provide, then it must be a sort of centeredness that isn't changed by life status or circumstances. Have you ever experienced that kind of peace? Think about or describe the circumstances. What would have to happen for you to experience that kind of peace in your life right now?

2. *"Don't worry about anything; instead, pray about everything. Tell God what you need, and thank him for all he has done. Then you will experience God's peace, which exceeds anything we can understand. His peace will guard your hearts and minds as you live in Christ Jesus"* (PHILIPPIANS 4:6-7).

a. In this verse are two actions we must take to partake of God's peace. The first is to tell Him what we need. Even though He knows our needs already, actually communicating them opens our hearts to receive His provision. Write down at least three current sources of worry in your life.

b. The second necessary action for experiencing God's peace is to thank Him for what He has done—articulating the ways He has been faithful in the past. We must reach into the past story of our journey with Jesus, take from that story the elements of God's faithfulness, and cast them into our current anxieties and future uncertainties. Write down one or two times (if any) in which you have experienced God's faithfulness in the past.

c. Using the two lists you have made, write down or say out loud a prayer for God's peace. Take a minute or two when you are through to meditate on the reality of God's nourishing peace. Then reflect: What was this experience like for you?

3. *"Abide in Me, and I in you. As the branch cannot bear fruit of itself unless it abides in the vine, so neither can you unless you abide in Me. I am the vine, you are the branches; he who abides in Me and I in him, he bears much fruit, for apart from Me you can do nothing"* (JOHN 15:4-5, NASB).

    a. Just as a vine spreads the nutrition it absorbs from the earth into each and every living branch, so Christ channels nourishment from the Father to us. Jesus longs for us to know Him as intimately as a branch knows the vine to which it is attached, depending on Him for our very lives. Abiding in Jesus is an act of complete reliance, an acknowledgment that we cannot live or flourish apart from Him, any more than a severed branch can grow and bloom. Do you think you abide in Christ this way? Why or why not? What is the difference between abiding in Him and simply being passive in life?

    b. We all need food and drink to survive physically, and in our spiritual lives we need the sustenance of the Spirit. Such "food" comes to us in all sorts of strange and wonderful ways: through the kindness of friends and family, in the beauty of a blazing sunset, in the gentle caress of music on our ears, in the words of Scripture, in the savory goodness of a lovingly prepared meal. What kind of experiences tend to feed your spirit? How can you put yourself in a position to receive the spiritual nourishment you need?

c. The proper response to a good meal prepared for you is enjoyment, appreciation, and thanksgiving. What does that tell you about the appropriate way to respond to Christ's gift of Himself for our nourishment? How can you best express your enjoyment of Him, your appreciation for His gifts to you, and your gratitude for His sustaining grace? Prayer is an important possibility, of course, but are there others?

CHAPTER 2

GOD SETS A TABLE EVERY DAY FOR OUR NEEDS

The whole community of Israel complained about Moses and Aaron.

"If only the LORD had killed us back in Egypt," they moaned.
"There we sat around pots filled with meat and ate all the bread we
wanted. But now you have brought us into this wilderness to starve
us all to death."

Then the LORD said to Moses, "Look, I'm going to rain down
food from heaven for you. Each day the people can go out and pick
up as much food as they need for that day. I will test them in this to
see whether or not they will follow my instructions. On the sixth day
they will gather food, and when they prepare it, there will be twice
as much as usual."

EXODUS 16:2-5

That evening the disciples came to [Jesus] and said, "This is a
remote place, and it's already getting late. Send the crowds away
so they can go to the villages and buy food for themselves."

But Jesus said, "That isn't necessary—you feed them."

"But we have only five loaves of bread and two fish!" they
answered.

"Bring them here," he said. Then he told the people to sit down

*on the grass. Jesus took the five loaves and two fish, looked up toward
heaven, and blessed them. Then, breaking the loaves into pieces, he
gave the bread to the disciples, who distributed it to the people. They
all ate as much as they wanted, and afterward, the disciples picked
up twelve baskets of leftovers. About 5,000 men were fed that day,
in addition to all the women and children!*

MATTHEW 14:15-21

Setting the Table

It is alarming how quickly life can transition from the miraculous to the mundane.

Just a few months earlier, the Israelites had been a captive people, working as slaves under the burning Egyptian sun. Then suddenly, in a swift and violent moment, things began to change. Ten plagues fell upon the Egyptians, the Israelites' oppressors. With each strike from the hand of God, Moses requested His people's release. Though they had nearly forgotten how, the Israelites began to hope. And finally, in the greatest drama of all, they escaped. The sea parted, they walked across the dry seabed, and then their pursuing enemies were swallowed up in the bitter salt water. And they sang—oh, how they sang!—of God's great deliverance.

But just a few days later everything was ordinary again. And the people were hungry. Perhaps the whole escape from Egypt was not so miraculous after all. Had they imagined the hand of God in it all? Maybe living in Egypt had been better.

What good is it to be free if you're only going to starve? And so their songs quickly turned to grumbles.

And it was not so different for the followers of Jesus.

Being with Him was a constant adventure. As they moved through the towns, miracles bloomed in their wake: healing, exorcisms, feasts where the wine never ran out. And Jesus' teaching seemed like its own kind of miracle. It rang with authority, delivered in the form of simple stories with endings that surprised and sometimes stung with conviction. In Him, people oppressed by the burdens of stringent priestly laws and government taxation found hope again.

But even in the midst of life-changing, world-altering events, blood-sugar levels drop, stomachs growl, and little ones cry for a snack. And everything suddenly seems very ordinary.

This experience of the miraculous fading into the mundane is common to the life of faith. Each of us in our own way can sense this pattern at some point in our walk with God. The passion following our conversion follows us for weeks, maybe even months or years, but somewhere along the way we find ourselves sleepy, tired, forgetful, and annoyed with our neighbor. God's mighty provision produces in us a boldness and a thankfulness, and we resolve to always live the life of faith— until we find ourselves wishing that just for once we would have enough in the bank that we didn't have to live by faith.

And so we wail at God in the desert.

We politely pull one of the disciples aside to ask, "When is lunch?"

One of the lessons that God's provision of manna and

Jesus' feeding of the five thousand can teach us is that God works not only in isolated, miraculous moments of our lives, but also in the day-to-day provision for our needs.

In these two scriptural stories, Old and New Testament, we see very human responses: hunger, annoyance, angst. We are reminded that to be human is to have a body, and to have a body is to be limited and to have needs. We sometimes respond to these facts with a doleful acceptance, but it is perhaps better to remember that this essential neediness is built into human nature by God to remind us that we are not self-sufficient. Just as we need food, sleep, and water, we need God. And we live better when we practice a joyful acceptance of this design in our lives, acknowledging our essential neediness, living in a spiritually and physically sustainable way, and presenting each need, each mundane moment, to God.

The bodies we live in and with remind us of another important spiritual reality: We need regular sustenance to live and to live well. One meal will not sustain us for an entire week or month; we must engage in the mundane task of preparing food and feeding ourselves a few times every day. And instead of sleeping once a week, we face the absurd necessity of lying prostrate, unconscious and vulnerable, for hours each day. This element of rhythmic neediness reminds us of an essential truth: At each moment, our being is dependent upon God.

In our walk with God, then, we cannot depend on an occasional quiet time or church service to sustain us. To live sustainably, we must learn to live according to the cadence of our need: for food, for sleep, for companionship, and especially for God. We must remember that He cares about these needs because they are essential to how He created us. He knows our limitations and delights to see us thrive.

When the Israelites were saved from the Egyptians, God did not ephemerally provide spiritual support for the Israelites. He provided them manna, a daily source of physical sustenance. Jesus did not only provide the crowd with spiritual teachings and admonitions. He fed them bread and fish—and they even had leftovers! God's will is to care for us as holistic beings, ministering to our hearts and our bodies in a consistent manner.

To flourish the way God created us to, we must use our wisdom and will to intentionally shape rhythms of life to sustain our souls and bodies, and we must remember to present every moment, issue, and concern to the God who cares for us. Practically speaking, this means developing a battle plan for rest, margin, food, and fun as well as worship. We must pay attention to the signs of our exhaustion. When we feel we are cratering, full of doubt or inexplicably grumpy, perhaps that feeling is not a sign of spiritual fallibility, but a signal from our souls and bodies that it is time to attend to the needs God has given us. To sleep, to eat, perhaps to enjoy tea with a friend—to partake of the daily manna of self-care that God enables us to pursue.

Beyond this, we must learn to live in daily surrender and conversation with God. In the same way that we nourish and rest our bodies daily, we must learn, day by day and moment by moment, to nourish our hearts on the presence of God.

In the same way we make time to eat and drink, we must make time to fill our souls spiritually. Do we have the same intentionality in pursuing God as we do pursuing lunch or our morning coffee? His care for us is not abstract, but personal and specific. The longer we walk in His presence, the easier it becomes to talk to Him each moment as we would talk to a friend we are completely comfortable with.

We all long for moments of the miraculous, but the life of faith is a marathon. So often the long work of faithfulness is accomplished not in moments of grandeur, but in the many mundane but grace-filled moments and days that come before and after. To live well, we must learn to be skillful conductors of our lives, living into a rhythmic sustainability, nurturing a dynamic relationship with God as we offer Him our every day and thought, and trusting in His provision and love.

Table Talk

CONVERSATION STARTERS

1. Are you the kind of person who thrives on routine, or do you struggle when life seems dull or mundane? Do you tend to neglect self-care? Do you get impatient with the day-in-day-outness of life? Why do you believe this is true for you?

2. What have been some of the high points of your spiritual life? What happened afterward? Have you personally experienced what this chapter describes— the fading of the miraculous into the ordinary?

3. What would change if you really believed that your daily needs (for nourishment, rest, and so on) are part of God's design?

4. Do you think God's people are called at times to rise above these daily needs—for instance, to fast or to respond to a crisis? How can we tell the difference?

DIGGING DEEPER

1. *"You make springs pour water into the ravines, so streams gush down from the mountains. They provide water for all the animals, and the wild donkeys quench their thirst. The birds nest beside the streams and sing among the branches of the trees. You send rain on the mountains from your heavenly home, and you fill the earth with the fruit of your labor. You cause grass to grow for the livestock and plants for people to use. You allow them to produce food from the earth—wine to make them glad, olive oil to soothe their skin, and bread to give them strength"* (PSALM 104:10-15).

   a. Read this psalm out loud at your table. The psalmist beautifully imagines the ways God sustains our individual lives and the life of all creation. What things in the natural world remind you of God's care and provision?

b. What is your favorite season? What can this current season teach about God's rhythms of provision?

c. Plan a time this week to take a walk in nature and dwell on God's continual provision for the world.

2. *"Pray like this: Our Father in heaven, may your name be kept holy. May your Kingdom come soon. May your will be done on earth, as it is in heaven. Give us today the food we need, and forgive us our sins, as we have forgiven those who sin against us. And don't let us yield to temptation, but rescue us from the evil one"* (MATTHEW 6:9-13).

a. This is the Lord's Prayer, prayed each week in many churches. It's what Jesus suggested when He was asked, "How should we pray?" Why do you think Jesus included the phrase "Give us today the food we need"? Why do you think it's important to specifically ask for God's provision of our everyday needs? Doesn't God already *know* what we need?

b. This prayer reminds us that our physical, emotional, and spiritual needs are important to God. Do you ever feel hesitant to pray about your everyday needs? Why or why not?

c. How might you be more intentional about tending to your everyday physical, emotional, and spiritual needs? What is a rhythm you could introduce into your life to live more sustainably?

3. *"Humble yourselves under the mighty power of God, and at the right time he will lift you up in honor. Give all your worries and cares to God, for he cares about you"* (1 PETER 5:6-7).

a. Peter notes that humility—humbling ourselves— is part of praying to God about our daily needs, worries, and cares. Why do you think this matters? In what ways could pride keep you from bringing God your worries and requests?

b. Do you ever forget to bring your cares to God? Why?

c. Peter tells us to bring our cares to God because God cares about us and our needs. But sometimes it is difficult to remember or imagine that the infinite God cares about our little worries. Is that true for you? If you really believed that the all-powerful God cares for your daily struggles, how would it change the way you live?

d. Write down two or three issues or concerns that seem too mundane for God to care about. Tell them to a friend or family member and ask them about their worries as well. Pray about them together.

CHAPTER 3

GOD NOURISHES AND RESTORES US

The angel of the LORD came again and touched him and said, "Get up and eat some more, or the journey ahead will be too much for you."

So he got up and ate and drank, and the food gave him enough strength to travel forty days and forty nights to Mount Sinai, the mountain of God.

1 KINGS 19:7-8

"Bring some of the fish you've just caught," Jesus said. So Simon Peter went aboard and dragged the net to the shore. There were 153 large fish, and yet the net hadn't torn.

"Now come and have some breakfast!" Jesus said. None of the disciples dared to ask him, "Who are you?" They knew it was the Lord. Then Jesus served them the bread and the fish.

JOHN 21:10-13

Setting the Table

Elijah had simply had too much. For such a long time he had fought against the idolatry of Ahab and Ahab's wicked queen, Jezebel, declaring the Lord's power against the pagan priests of Baal. Four hundred and fifty had been slain through God's miraculous intervention, the culmination of Elijah's prophetic witness. But now, even after multiple miracles, Elijah found himself running for his life from Jezebel's wrath.

Storm after storm he had weathered, but now he was growing weary. Would his life with the Lord ever involve anything but service and obedience? Would there never be a respite from the onslaught of wickedness? All the victories he had known seemed to amount to nothing. Evil still triumphed, and it hounded him relentlessly through a barren desert. He could see nothing but the heavy cloud of his despair, and surely the fatigue of his flight only added to that sense of hopelessness.

Eventually he collapsed beneath a broom tree and gave up. "I have had enough, Lord," he said. "Take my life, for I am no better than my ancestors who have already died."

Elijah would have had good company in the apostle Peter. Peter found himself similarly staring into a void of emptiness. After the years of ministry with Jesus, he found himself exactly back where he had started, laboring as a lowly fisherman trying to bring in a catch of fish that simply wouldn't be found. Each toss of the net into the vacant water reminded him of what had come to naught. All those miracles of

Jesus—ordinary water transformed into the highest-quality wine at a wedding, astounding meals for massive crowds from a few modest loaves and fish, people healed, Lazarus raised from the dead—what did any of that matter now?

Even Peter's own hope for a life filled with meaning, a purpose beyond his small place in the world, seemed to be slipping away. In the Master, he had seen life become something beyond what he'd been able to imagine with his limited view of the world. Jesus talked often of a coming Kingdom, the arrival of God into the midst of the struggles the Jewish people labored under with Roman oppression. He had thought he'd caught the vision. But then Jesus had been executed like a common criminal. And even worse, Peter had failed miserably, denying Jesus in his Lord's moment of need. There was nothing left but to strive aimlessly after elusive answers, to seek after a catch that simply wouldn't be found.

Both Elijah and Peter desperately needed God to restore them to their vital ministries. Both teetered on the edge of the abyss of despair, ready to give up their calling and diminish into nothingness. They were spiritually starved, aching with hunger for the life of the Spirit, which had flowed so powerfully through them at one point in their lives.

God saw both men in their need, and in His faithfulness He did intervene. They would each receive a definitive call back into ministry and be set back on firm ground to move forward with the call of the Lord upon them. But that call would start with something much simpler, something much more fundamental.

It started with a meal.

For Elijah, it took the form of bread and water and restful sleep. His vision on Mount Sinai was coming, but the Lord saw and met his physical need first, knowing the sustenance would prepare him for the spiritual calling to come. For Peter, it came as a delectable meal of roasted fish and bread, fish that Peter had longed to catch and that Jesus finally brought in miraculous abundance. Before He restored Peter the apostle to ministry, He renewed Peter the fisherman, both in his physical work of fishing and in his physical need for food.

When Jesus sends us out into the world, He prepares a meal for us first. He serves our most basic needs before He commissions us. God is faithful to restore our ideals and our desire to serve Him and His Kingdom. But first He desires us to eat and drink and be comforted.

God is not unaware of our needs. He sees our whole selves—body, soul, and spirit. Yes, He seeks our worship of Him in mind and spirit, but He carefully crafted our minds to need food and water to function properly. God delights in how He created us; from the beginning, He declared that what He made was "very good." God Himself ordained that our spiritual well-being and our physical strength would be inexorably bound to each other.

Could God transcend the limits of time and space to miraculously accomplish His spiritual ends? It's certainly possible; we know that He is Lord over all creation. And yet our very salvation came through God becoming human. As the Lord of creation, He deigned to wear our flesh, fusing His eternal being with the stuff of our created universe. And then He gave that very body as a sacrifice to save us. The story the Gospels present to us is about a God who came in bodily form and shared in our weaknesses and sufferings, who Himself cried out on the cross, "I am thirsty." He himself experienced those fundamental human needs, so He knows what it's like to need restoration in body and soul.

Perhaps even now you are fatigued and feeling low. Perhaps you are hungry or thirsty, and you feel the weight of the world pressing down on you. Perhaps the Lord longs simply to provide for your needs with food, drink, and rest as He did with His beloved children Elijah and Peter. Whatever troubles you, He sees you and is there for you.

Today, accept the Lord's blessing through a meal or a cup of something refreshing. Find Him in rest and sleep. As you partake in the rhythms of food and fellowship and rest, He will draw you into a closer walk with Him and into the callings upon your life.

It all begins with a meal.

Table Talk

CONVERSATION STARTERS

1. Describe a time when you were physically or mentally depleted. How did that affect your spiritual well-being? How did you find refreshment and restoration (if you did)?

2. Do you tend to discount or neglect your physical needs for nourishment and rest? Why or why not?

3. If God uses food and drink to restore our bodies, why do you think He also tells us to fast at times?

4. How does Jesus' command to feed the hungry echo with the themes of this passage? How does this relate to missions and evangelism?

DIGGING DEEPER

1. *"That is why I tell you not to worry about everyday life— whether you have enough food and drink, or enough clothes to wear. Isn't life more than food, and your body more than clothing? Look at the birds. They don't plant or harvest or store food in barns, for your heavenly Father feeds them. And aren't you far more valuable to him than they are? Can all your worries add a single moment to your life?"* (MATTHEW 6:25-27).

   a. Of all the temptations we face day-to-day, one of the most pressing and repeated is the temptation to fear that God won't provide and that therefore we must strain and stress to take care of ourselves. Write down at least three needs you have that tend to raise this kind of fear in you. Why do you think these needs cause you so much anxiety?

b. What does this verse tell you about how God sees us and provides for us? What does it tell you about your fears and your anxiety and the way you approach God for help?

c. This verse also tells us specifically that worry doesn't help us one bit. What do you typically worry about? What are some practical alternatives to worry? How can you learn to rest in God's peace and provision and seek Him in expectancy?

2. *"I do not need the bulls from your barns or the goats from your pens. For all the animals of the forest are mine, and I own the cattle on a thousand hills. . . . Make thankfulness your sacrifice to God, and keep the vows you made to the Most High. Then call on me when you are in trouble, and I will rescue you, and you will give me glory"* (PSALM 50:9-10, 14-15).

a. It is tempting to think that if we work hard or accomplish a certain amount in a given day, week, month, or year, then we will have earned God's favor.

But this passage rebuffs that idea altogether. God has the very power of the universe at His fingertips. He needs nothing from us but our trust in Him. What are some ways you are tempted to "do" for God in order to win His favor?

b. When you come to God with your needs, what is your attitude? Do you begin with thankfulness? This passage suggests that instead of coming to God in fear that He won't provide, we should instead praise Him in anticipation of the ways in which He *will* provide. To practice this, take the list of needs and worries you created in the previous section. For each item on the list, praise God in your own words for the way in which He will take care of you. Then reflect: What difference does praying this way make to you?

3. *This same God who takes care of me will supply all your needs from his glorious riches, which have been given to us in Christ Jesus* (PHILIPPIANS 4:19).

a. The apostle Paul wants the Philippians to know here that God took care of him, so they can know God will take care of them as well. When you are tempted to worry, it helps to think of the people you know who have walked along the path for a longer time than you, who may have experienced what you are experiencing and can guide or reassure you. Who are some of those people in your life? (If you can't think of any, what steps could you take to connect with such mentors?)

b. Who is our perfect scriptural example of trusting God for our needs? What can we learn from the example of this person?

CHAPTER 4

NOW AND AT THE END OF TIME

The next day there was a wedding celebration in the village of Cana in Galilee. Jesus' mother was there, and Jesus and his disciples were also invited to the celebration. The wine supply ran out during the festivities, so Jesus' mother told him, "They have no more wine."

"Dear woman, that's not our problem," Jesus replied. "My time has not yet come."

But his mother told the servants, "Do whatever he tells you."

Standing nearby were six stone water jars, used for Jewish ceremonial washing. Each could hold twenty to thirty gallons. Jesus told the servants, "Fill the jars with water." When the jars had been filled, he said, "Now dip some out, and take it to the master of ceremonies." So the servants followed his instructions.

When the master of ceremonies tasted the water that was now wine, not knowing where it had come from (though, of course, the servants knew), he called the bridegroom over. "A host always serves the best wine first," he said. "Then, when everyone has had a lot to drink, he brings out the less expensive wine. But you have kept the best until now!"

This miraculous sign at Cana in Galilee was the first time Jesus revealed his glory. And his disciples believed in him.

JOHN 2:1-11

Setting the Table

Jesus loved weddings. And this one was particularly joyful.

The room was full to bursting with people, food, flowers, and laughter. A rich, smoky fragrance wafted through the air, evidence of the sumptuous feast that had been weeks in the making. Jesus smiled and clapped Simon on the back as He gleefully popped an olive into His mouth.

The whole community was there, celebrating, laughing, and singing prayers of blessing over the young couple. In a world so weighed down by oppressive laws and taxes and a hopeless political situation, it was good to see such unqualified happiness. Momentarily drawn away from the cacophonous joy, Jesus thought to Himself that His time had nearly come—not for the consummation of a marriage, but for His ministry to commence.

It was just at this moment that, over the clinking of glasses and roar of mirth, Jesus caught His mother's eye. Mary raised her eyebrows in a meaningful way, grinning slightly. With a pointed nod of her head, she turned her gaze toward the doorway to the kitchen. There stood the master of ceremonies, addressing a line of apologetic-looking servants in a frantic and frustrated manner.

Mary fixed her eyes again on Jesus. He recognized—and honored—that look of fervent but almost mischievous seriousness. He made His way over to where she stood.

"They have no more wine," said Mary matter-of-factly.

"Dear woman, that's not our problem," Jesus said with

a smile, gently grabbing Mary's hand. She was unperturbed but unconvinced.

"My time has not yet come," said Jesus with a bit more emphasis.

Mary nodded almost imperceptibly and made her way to the flustered servants. It was an embarrassment for this new couple to run out of wine for their wedding party—an ominous way to begin a marriage. Mary, however, had her eye on the situation.

"Do whatever He tells you," said Mary, looking over her shoulder at Jesus.

Jesus almost laughed. Mary was not to be defied, even by her holy Son.

Perhaps it was His time after all.

As Jesus made His way to the servants, Mary watched with a quiet thankfulness and joy. This Son of hers, whom she knew to be the Messiah, whom she had borne in her body and delivered into the world, was such a mystery and a grace to her. She smiled with the humble pride of a parent who is glad for the gift of their child.

The servants left the room and reentered with six jars. One drew a cup from a jar and took it to the fretting master of ceremonies, whose hand was draped across his face in worry. Impatiently he took a sip. Like a sudden spring thaw, his face melted from hardened concern to bewildered mirth. He hastened to the bridegroom and gestured wildly, "You've saved the best wine for last!"

Mary took a deep breath. Of course He would begin His

ministry this way, with a feast. Wasn't it always that way with God?

"The LORD *. . . will spread a wonderful feast for all the people of the world. . . ."*

She treasured these words from Isaiah, pondering them in her heart as she watched Jesus with wonder.

And so her Son began to spread the feast.

So much of life is waiting.

When we are children, we wait impatiently to be old enough to go to school, to ride the roller coaster, to sit in the front seat. As teens we wait to drive, to graduate, to fall in love. As adults we wait to get a good job, to get married, to have babies, to have grandchildren, to retire. We reach moments of fulfillment and perhaps even celebrate them, but there is always something else to wait for. Life is accompanied by an ongoing desire to arrive at some final point, some ultimate future.

The good news of Scripture is that someday—dare we believe it?—that future will arrive. And in Jesus, we already have a glimpse of that final satisfaction. We taste something of its sweetness as we walk through this present life with the Lord. But Scripture tells us we won't experience it fully until the end of time, when Jesus returns. Until the day when death reigns no more and all is made new.

In his poem "What the Bird Said Early in the Year," C. S. Lewis describes this future time as the day when "summer will come true."[2] There will come a day when the sudden rush of joy that comes with the long-awaited summer will be permanent, when peace will reign at last.

Someday. But not yet.

The tension of our lives is learning to live well in the waiting.

In the story of Jesus and the wedding feast, we are presented with rich truths of living in the tension of hope, faithfulness, and gratitude. Jesus' actions at the wedding feast and His consequent initiation of ministry invite us into a patient and celebratory feast that prefigures our hopes for God's final renewal of all things. Through this passage we are given a picture of how to live in light of the feast Jesus has already set before us while looking forward to the spectacular feast we have been promised.

Jesus' story begins in the context of waiting. For a Jewish couple in the first century, engagements could be up to four years long, as the bridegroom worked to show the bride's family he was ready to support her. A wedding celebration was accompanied by a great sigh of relief; the couple could begin their lives together at last.

We see quickly that Jesus had been waiting as well. So much is encompassed in His simple words to Mary: "My time has not yet come." When reading the Gospels, it is easy to think of Jesus' life as jam-packed with action, with never a moment when He wasn't healing or preaching. And yet Jesus lived a life of relative obscurity until age thirty. Outside the lens of the Gospel writers' view, He spent a majority of His life living, working, and waiting—just as we do—until it was time for His public ministry to begin.

Luke neatly sums up these invisible years of Jesus' life in one sentence: "Jesus grew in wisdom and in stature and in favor with God and all the people" (Luke 2:52). Surely those hidden years were not wasted, just as our unremarkable years are not wasted. Meditating for a moment on the many years that Jesus lived without any large consequence affirms to us God's regard for the quiet and faithful life.

As we wait and hope in life, let us not lose sight of the deep value of each ordinary day. Yet the foundation for our faithful days—the reason we can remain faithful—is the hope of the feast to come and the revelation of God's glory.

As Christians, we live in the already and the not yet. Jesus has already started the feast, and we can already taste the future fulfillment of our hopes, but that day has not yet arrived. The anticipated Savior of all has come and freed us from sin and death, but sin and death have not yet been banished from the world. We are still waiting.

It is worth dwelling on how the "already" aspects of our faith shape our lives. Jesus did change the water into wine; He did teach, heal, and live. He did die on a cross, and He did rise again. He has already sent the Holy Spirit to dwell in the hearts of His followers. Evidence of His Kingdom breaking out around the world is easy to see for those who have eyes to see. But there is still so much pain and brokenness. So much sin. So much waiting.

Jesus has already hosted one feast—the Last Supper with His disciples. He sets a new one regularly in our churches, when we follow His words and share bread and wine among us. He lays a banquet of life before us each morning as He waits to bless us with His love and the beauty of His world. But we can't help hungering for more—for a greater feast. And it is coming.

In beginning His ministry with a wedding feast, Jesus showed His own life to be an inauguration of God's redeeming work that will end in the great wedding feast of the Lamb (Revelation 19:6-9). The wedding feast Jesus attended at Cana is a foreshadowing of the feast of the Lamb, which surely will be bigger, better, more joyful, and more delicious than the most sumptuous banquet we can imagine here on earth.

The hope of that beautiful day can give our mundane days a purpose and direction because it gives us an eternal perspective. It keeps us aware of how intricately He works in our everyday lives, how important they all are. It helps us endure dark and difficult days and do the right but difficult thing one more time. And it reminds us that each moment of joy we experience is a taste of the glory for which we are made.

Life is full of waiting, but our waiting can be full of meaning. Like the couple who patiently waits to begin their life together, like Jesus living quietly in anticipation of His ministry's commencement, we can learn to live well as we wait.

We do this by recognizing the meaning of each ordinary day, knowing that God honors our faithfulness. We must also consider what it means to live in the light of the feast Jesus has already set for us—His ministry, His teaching, His sacrifice, and His ongoing presence. Finally, we learn to live with the promise of that final and best of feasts alive in our hearts.

I can't wait for that day. Can you?

Table Talk

CONVERSATION STARTERS

1. Describe some significant times of waiting in your life. What were you waiting for?

2. Why do you think waiting is so difficult for most of us? What helps make it better?

3. In your view, is patience always a virtue? What's the best way to know when to wait and when to act?

4. What experiences in your own life have offered you a taste of what God has in store for His people in the future? How have those moments helped you live well in the waiting?

DIGGING DEEPER

1. *"In Jerusalem, the LORD of Heaven's Armies will spread a wonderful feast for all the people of the world. It will be a delicious banquet with clear, well-aged wine and choice meat. There he will remove the cloud of gloom, the shadow of death that hangs over the earth. He will swallow up death forever! The Sovereign LORD will wipe away all tears.*

He will remove forever all insults and mockery against his land and people. . . . In that day the people will proclaim, 'This is our God! We trusted in him, and he saved us! This is the LORD, in whom we trusted. Let us rejoice in the salvation he brings!'" (ISAIAH 25:6-9).

a. What a beautiful picture Isaiah paints of the hope God gives us! What stands out to you about the feast Isaiah describes? What do you most look forward to about God's great feast for all the people of the world? The delicious food and drink? Meeting all of the nations and peoples of the world around one table? Saying good-bye for good to tears and death? Something else?

b. Why do you think it is important to keep the hope of God's eventual redemption of all things alive in our minds? Do you think dwelling on the future distracts us from the present? Or does it help us live with more purpose and hope in the present? Maybe a little of both? How does thinking about this future affect you?

2. *"Do not despise these small beginnings, for the LORD rejoices to see the work begin"* (ZECHARIAH 4:10).

    a. This passage was written regarding someone who began a work of God but would not see it completed in his lifetime. He is reminded that the small beginnings, those faithful acts that may not seem extraordinary, are precious to God. Jesus certainly modeled the importance of small beginnings in His own life. What circumstances in your life seem like "small beginnings" to you—inadequate and unlikely to bear much fruit? How might you commit them to God's glory?

    b. There are some acts of faithfulness that we may never see the consequences of in our lifetimes. What keeps you living faithfully and hopefully even when you can't see the final product? How do you keep God's hope alive in your heart?

3. *"I am certain that God, who began the good work within you, will continue his work until it is finally finished on the day when Christ Jesus returns"* (PHILIPPIANS 1:6).

    a. The work that began in your life when you became a Christian is a work that begins with God's provision, continues with God's supervision, and will be completed in God's future, when all things are made new. It is a natural tendency to worry about where we are in life and what the future holds. Do you find it easy to trust in God's grander story, knowing that He sees what is coming and holds you in His hand every day? Why or why not?

    b. Sometimes when it is difficult to catch that bigger vision, it is helpful to put down "memorial stones"— records of God's grace and provision in our lives. One way to do this is by keeping a journal or notebook. When you go to sleep at night, write down three small or large ways you've seen God work toward sanctification in your life or redemption in the world around you. Praise God specifically for those things and ask Him to show you more examples every day.

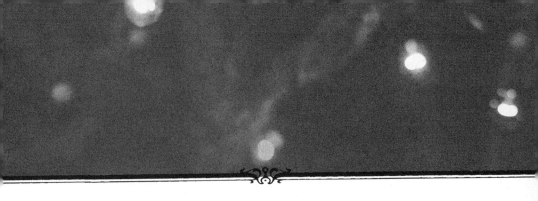

PART 2

We Prepare a Table for God

CHAPTER 5

IT'S ABOUT THE GUEST, NOT THE HOST

Now as they went on their way, Jesus entered a village. And a woman named Martha welcomed him into her house. And she had a sister called Mary, who sat at the Lord's feet and listened to his teaching. But Martha was distracted with much serving. And she went up to him and said, "Lord, do you not care that my sister has left me to serve alone? Tell her then to help me." But the Lord answered her, "Martha, Martha, you are anxious and troubled about many things, but one thing is necessary. Mary has chosen the good portion, which will not be taken away from her."

LUKE 10:38-42, ESV

Setting the Table

Martha was intent on being prepared. The Master was coming to her house, and she would finally have a chance to show Him the hospitality He deserved. Along with her sister, Mary, and their brother, Lazarus, Martha had followed Jesus throughout His ministry, being transformed first in spirit, then through the bond of friendship. Martha treasured that friendship with Jesus. Not only had He brought goodness and purpose into the life of her family; He had also given Martha personally a sense of value. In inviting Jesus to her home, she felt she could show Him her gratitude by using her gifts to their fullest extent. She would be the perfect host.

She had tried to draw her family into the happenings as well. As the eldest of their little household, Martha took her responsibility for her family very seriously. She wanted to encourage her siblings to consider their responsibilities in their home as an expression of their worship to God and their thankfulness for the Master's presence in their lives. And Mary had been helpful enough before Jesus arrived. But as soon as the rabble of ragtag disciples descended upon their little home, Mary had quickly been whisked into their world and forgotten all about her responsibilities. It was so typical of Mary to be this way. Whenever Jesus came into the picture, she lost all perspective and simply fawned at His feet.

It was unfair, really. Of course Martha wanted to listen in with everyone as well, to enjoy Jesus' presence. But she had worked so hard to craft a hospitable evening, and even if Mary abandoned her, she would stick to the task. Surely Jesus would see what a beautiful feast she had prepared and appreciate all the work she had done to make Him happy.

She checked the stew over the fire to see if it had reached the appropriate heat, accidentally burning her hand on the edge of the pot as she did. Just then a laugh rose up from the next room. Everyone was sharing in a humorous moment, and she was being left out. Suddenly she felt the heat of anger rise up within her as the searing burn from the pot throbbed with pain. Here she had gone to such immense trouble to prepare a delicious meal for Jesus, and no one was paying attention. They were all having a good time without her. And Mary was in there enjoying the Master's presence, instead of helping Martha. It really *was* unfair. Surely the Lord would see that.

She marched into the room, and to her consternation she saw Mary at the very center of the room, at Jesus' feet, staring up like a wide-eyed fawn. Martha's anger was starting to boil over. This was their opportunity to prove their gratitude to the Master by being consummate hosts, and there was Mary being completely useless, not showing the Master any hospitality at all.

Jesus was in the middle of saying something, but before Martha could stop herself, the words poured out of her mouth, cutting Him off midsentence. "Lord, doesn't it seem unfair to You that my sister just sits here while I do all the work? Tell her to come and help me!"

There was a sudden awkward silence as Jesus regarded Martha. Instead of speaking to Mary, He continued to look straight at Martha, compassion in His eyes. "My dear Martha, you are worried and upset over all these details! There is only one thing worth being concerned about. Mary has discovered it, and it will not be taken away from her."

Martha felt ashamed. Chastened. What she had desired for

her sister to feel, she was now experiencing. She didn't understand. She had wanted to prove her worth to Jesus, for Him to recognize the value in her preparations and her desire to serve Him. But instead of His approval, she had received His rebuke. His tone had been gentle, but the words still stung.

Jesus gently gestured to a spot next to Mary. Feeling confused and deflated, Martha sat down next to her sister and finally began to listen. And that made all the difference.

You see, Martha had thought her worth before the Lord lay in her own good motives, her hospitality skills, her power as a host. She thought she could prove to the Lord her value by using her gifts, the very gifts given to her by Jesus Himself. She imagined that after all the Lord had done for her and her family, she could initiate something in return.

In Jesus' economy, however, inviting Him in means focusing on who He is, not on who we are or what we want—even if what we want is a good thing like showing our love. It's not about what a good host we are, but rather, what a good guest Jesus is.

Does this mean that Martha's hard work was all a waste? Of course not. It wasn't a matter of preparation, but rather a matter of priorities. In Martha's heart, what Jesus had to say was subordinate to what she had to offer Him. She wanted to prove her value when Jesus had already affirmed that value through His presence in her home.

Jesus Himself is the gift through which we are able to enjoy our own gifting. It is through Him first, and His love for us, that we are able to enjoy serving Him—not because we have anything to prove to Him but because He already delights in us.

Today, as you seek the Lord, are there areas you are focusing on to try to make His presence in your life worthwhile? Be encouraged that there is nothing you can do to prove the rightness of Jesus residing within you. Don't worry too much about being the consummate host; He loves you already and is making His home within you. Take comfort in His deep approval for you, in the beauty of the heavenly Guest residing in your heart. Then you will find delight in seeing the good in your life and expressing it with love.

Table Talk

CONVERSATION STARTERS

1. Do you remember a time from your childhood when someone (a teacher, a parent, a sibling) treated you unfairly? What was the circumstance? How did you react?

2. Do you tend to identify more with Mary or with Martha?

3. What kinds of things do you tend to do really well? How do you typically arrange your days in order to use those skills?

4. What would be a modern equivalent of sitting at Jesus' feet?

Digging Deeper

1. *"God saved you by his grace when you believed. And you can't take credit for this; it is a gift from God. Salvation is not a reward for the good things we have done, so none of us can boast about it"* (Ephesians 2:8-9).

   a. What are your gifts? What are the things you hold on to that you feel give you value? Make a little list of these. Then consider: Do you tend to lean too much toward exercising those gifts to make you feel good about yourself—even in God's service—rather than focusing on the One who gave you these gifts and letting your time with Him be your first focus?

   b. Do you have a hard time believing that God desires your simple presence more than your dedicated service? Why or why not? What would change about your life if you took this reality to heart? What would help you trust in His grace more often rather than working to impress Him?

2. *"Do nothing from selfish ambition or conceit, but in humility count others more significant than yourselves. . . . Have this mind among yourselves, which is yours in Christ Jesus, who, though he was in the form of God, did not count equality with God a thing to be grasped, but emptied himself, by taking the form of a servant, being born in the likeness of men. And being found in human form, he humbled himself by becoming obedient to the point of death, even death on a cross. Therefore God has highly exalted him and bestowed on him the name that is above every name"* (PHILIPPIANS 2:3, 5-9, ESV).

   a. What is the key difference between Martha's kind of service as evidenced at her dinner party and Jesus' example of service as described in this verse? What does this tell us about how we must learn to serve as we follow Him?

   b. Are there people in your life who are difficult for you to relate to? Do you have friends or family members who test your patience or whom you find it difficult to forgive? List one or two of these. Why do you think these particular people bother you so much? How can the description of Jesus

THE LIFEGIVING TABLE EXPERIENCE

in this verse help you in relating to the problem people in your life?

c. Does humbling ourselves to serve mean it's never okay to voice our frustrations or confront someone who has wronged us? Why or why not? What is the best way to handle our struggles with other people?

3. *"He said, 'My grace is all you need. My power works best in weakness.' So now I am glad to boast about my weaknesses, so that the power of Christ can work through me"* (2 CORINTHIANS 12:9).

a. It is so tempting to say, "God, You can have all these many areas of my life, but not *that* one. You can only have that weakness if You take it away." But God is in the business of using our weaknesses and showing His power *through* them. Can you think of a time in the past when Jesus used one of your flaws or failings to accomplish something you never expected? List any areas of your life that you feel are broken beyond repair. Pray that God will give you the grace to allow

Jesus to work through your brokenness and change you day by day.

b. Write down a flaw or weakness in your life that really bothers you. Are you ever tempted to push past that weakness yourself through sheer willpower? Have you tried? What has been the result so far? What do you think would happen if you stopped trying to eliminate or change that weakness and instead gave Jesus permission to work through the weakness to change *you*?

c. As you seek the Lord this week, memorize this verse and make it part of your day-to-day prayers. Whenever you feel you have messed up or find yourself frustrated by a weakness in your life, stop and repeat it as your gospel truth. Don't be afraid to repeat it as many times throughout the day as is necessary to make it real in your life.

CHAPTER 6

TAKING TIME TO FEAST IN EXILE

On the tenth day of this month each family must choose a lamb or a young goat for a sacrifice. . . .

Take special care of this chosen animal until the evening of the fourteenth day of this first month. Then the whole assembly of the community of Israel must slaughter their lamb or young goat at twilight. They are to take some of the blood and smear it on the sides and top of the doorframes of the houses where they eat the animal. That same night they must roast the meat over a fire and eat it along with bitter salad greens and bread made without yeast. Do not eat any of the meat raw or boiled in water. The whole animal— including the head, legs, and internal organs—must be roasted over a fire. Do not leave any of it until the next morning. Burn whatever is not eaten before morning.

These are your instructions for eating this meal: Be fully dressed, wear your sandals, and carry your walking stick in your hand. Eat the meal with urgency, for this is the LORD's Passover. On that night I will pass through the land of Egypt and strike down every firstborn son and firstborn male animal. . . . I will execute judgment against all the gods of Egypt, for I am the LORD! But the blood on your doorposts will serve as a sign,

*marking the houses where you are staying. When I see the blood,
I will pass over you. This plague of death will not touch you
when I strike the land of Egypt.*

*This is a day to remember. Each year, from generation to
generation, you must celebrate it as a special festival to the LORD.
This is a law for all time. For seven days the bread you eat must be
made without yeast. On the first day of the festival, remove every
trace of yeast from your homes. . . . This Festival of Unleavened
Bread . . . will be a permanent law for you; celebrate this day from
generation to generation.*

EXODUS 12:3, 6-15, 17

Setting the Table

The Lord had spoken, and all the Israelites had heard the
decree. A new feast had been established, a feast celebrating
the Lord's promise to deliver His people from the oppression
of the Egyptians. Each family was to sacrifice a young goat or
lamb, spread its blood on the doorframe of their house, and
then eat the beast whole after cooking it over a fire. The whole
community was adjured to remember the moment in future
years by refraining from leavened bread for seven days and
removing all yeast from their houses. In this way, the Israelites
would honor the Lord, and He would pass over their houses,
even as He killed the firstborn of each Egyptian household.

It was undoubtedly a strange kind of feast, but it was
matched to an equally strange set of circumstances. All around

them, plagues and pestilence were laying the land bare. The land of Egypt, where they lived as foreign slaves, was in complete disorder, and chaos reigned everywhere. The Egyptians were dangerously angry, held back from harming the Israelites only by a greater fear of the God who had already smitten them with a multitude of calamities. The whole Israelite community was in survival mode, ready to flee for their very lives from the agitated and unpredictable Egyptian people. And here, right in the middle of the madness, God was asking them to stop and make a feast?

The tension had been growing ever since Moses and Aaron had first come and boldly commanded that the Pharaoh let their people go. The Egyptian king had simply laughed. He had waved his hand dismissively and scoffed at the elderly Jewish men. "Moses and Aaron, why are you distracting the people from your tasks? Get back to work!" Then, to add insult to injury, the old tyrant had immediately punished the Israelites by forcing them to create bricks without the straw necessary to hold the mud together.

But the Lord was watching, and the oppression of His people would not remain unanswered. First came the blood. All the water in Egypt turned a sickening red, a death stroke against all the fish in the Nile and a devastation to the supply of clean drinking water. Next came the frogs. Covering the streets and intruding in hoards upon living spaces, the vile creatures disgusted the Egyptians in a nightmare of amphibious infestation. Soon afterward, gnats took their turn to torment the Egyptians, and then flies ravaged the land with a tempestuous fury. Again and again the Lord sent His judgment on the Egyptian people, and each time the stubborn pharaoh refused to listen. Not even after the indignity and pain of a sickness that left the population ravaged by boils would he relent.

The whole land was at a tipping point, and the Israelites could feel it like a palpable, noxious fog creeping along the way. Even a little more suffering, and chaos might reign. And now this same God bringing down vengeance against Egypt was calling them to wait, keep vigil, and celebrate their coming liberation by sharing a meal together.

It was indeed strange—and wonderful. The inbreaking of the Holy into the unbroken normal of five hundred years of oppression. A sacred spilling of justice into the profane slavery the Israelites had known for so long. God not only intended to liberate His people from the evil of Egyptian rule; He intended also to sanctify them for that coming freedom.

And how did the Passover meal accomplish such a grand feat?

First, the Passover engendered a deep trust in God's provision. God's command to sacrifice a whole young lamb or goat and to cook and eat every part of it was spoken to an impoverished people, living hand to mouth. To prepare so generous a feast meant trusting completely and fully that God would not only provide for their day-to-day needs, but would also liberate them into the fullness of abundant life in Him.

In addition, preparing and partaking in such a meal at God's command would reinforce their awareness that they were His people—sanctified, set apart. When the Israelites would reenact the feast every year after that first fateful night in Egypt, they would remember that just as they removed the yeast from their homes, God removed the sin from their hearts and made them holy vessels.

And so it is for us today. Preparing a meal in the presence of God is still, in a certain sense, an acknowledgment that the Lord provides the food we need. We can enjoy eating because we understand that all our provision first comes from God and that our practice of feasting is a sacrifice of praise back to Him. And preparing and partaking in such a meal at God's command is also to heed His call to sanctification. It is to accept His sign upon the doorposts not just of our houses, but of our innermost parts—in the words of Proverbs 3:3, to write God's commandments "deep within" our hearts. It is a recognition that God desires to make of us something new, something that represents His holiness in the world.

Today, as you consider the busyness of your life or find yourself overwhelmed with the challenges, difficulties, or sorrows that press down upon you, take time to share a holy moment with others. Eat a meal, share it with friends and family, and remember in that small action that God provides for and longs to give abundantly to His children. Remember also that as we feast in the midst of the darkness around us, we are proclaiming that God's light burns brighter than any difficulty that might stand in our path. Feasting is a declaration that we believe forward into God's desire for us not only to survive, but to thrive and to move into His liberating life.

Take time today to remember that the sacred enters our

lives not just when we are prepared for it, but when we stop amid the whirlwind and celebrate, when we feast "in the presence of [our] enemies," as the psalmist says (Psalm 23:5). God is ready to surprise us with the gift of His profound goodness if only we would stop—and feast.

Table Talk

CONVERSATION STARTERS

1. What do you think was strange or unusual about the feast that God instructed His people to share?

2. At what times of your life have you felt overwhelmed by circumstances?

3. Do you find it difficult to think of feasting or celebrating when your circumstances are difficult or overwhelming? Why or why not?

4. What are some ways you can approach your mealtimes differently in order to keep you and your family aware of God's provision and call to a new life in Him?

DIGGING DEEPER

1. *"You prepare a feast for me in the presence of my enemies. You honor me by anointing my head with oil. My cup overflows with blessings"* (PSALM 23:5).

   a. Are you hesitant to partake of the Lord's grace in your life until the whirlwind around you ceases? Go ahead and feast! God's abundant blessing is everywhere for us, even in the midst of uncertainty or trouble. Write down the things that you feel you have been waiting to seek out as blessings because of your circumstances. Pray that the Lord will allow you to receive grace well, even in difficult seasons.

b. Do you feel your cup isn't overflowing right now? Do you feel more of the drought than the plenty of the land? God wants you to know His abundant love and grace right now in the midst of your time of trial. He's waiting in hidden places all around for you to find Him and delight in Him. If you are in a place of drought right now, do those things that typically give you peace or happiness. Enjoy a cup of tea or coffee. Go outside and soak in nature. Read a good book or listen to music that speaks to your soul. Attend a concert or a poetry reading. Take a run or a long bike ride. Seek God's presence in the beautiful things around you, no matter what is happening in your life. Then you, too, will be able to feast in the presence of your "enemies."

2. *"Praise the LORD! Praise God in his sanctuary; praise him
    in his mighty heavens! Praise him for his mighty deeds;
    praise him according to his excellent greatness! Praise him
    with trumpet sound; praise him with lute and harp! Praise
    him with tambourine and dance; praise him with strings
    and pipe! Praise him with sounding cymbals; praise him
    with loud clashing cymbals! Let everything that has breath
    praise the LORD! Praise the LORD!"* (PSALM 150, ESV).

    a. Did you know that simply praising God can raise
       your spirits? When you praise God, that small act
       has the power to shine the light of God's presence
       even in the darkest corners of your life. If, like
       the Israelites in Egypt, you are fearful of what is
       happening around you, start with praise—right
       here, right now. Sing a hymn, read a praise psalm
       (like the one above) out loud, or use your own
       words of praise.

    b. How creative is your worship? Do you relegate
       your praise only to prayer or to "spiritual" actions?
       The psalmist wants us to know there are limit-
       less ways to praise God over the regular course
       of our lives. Write down three normal things you
       will do today—from washing dishes to having a

conversation with a friend or family member. Plan to engage your will toward praise when you do those things and watch how God will meet you in your worship.

3. *"I gave them my Sabbath days of rest as a sign between them and me. It was to remind them that I am the LORD, who had set them apart to be holy"* (EZEKIEL 20:12).

   a. Just as God called the Israelites to observe the Passover, so He calls us to observe His Sabbath—not because God needs our observance, but because *we* need it. We fulfill our purpose when we rest in Him and delight in Him. By observing a regular time of rest in the midst of our busy, overwhelming lives, we recognize that God is the one who provides us with true peace and that our striving will accomplish nothing if it is not rooted in God's work in our lives. Is that Sabbath rest part of your life? What would need to happen for it to become so?

b. For a limited period of time—say, six weeks—try keeping a personal Sabbath. It doesn't have to be Sunday. In fact, church commitments may make it difficult for you to truly rest on Sunday. But set aside a day or at least several hours once a week for a time of rest, reflection, and worship. Try to remove any commitments or projects or busyness from this time. If you do anything, make it gentle and restorative— light reading, a walk outdoors, a simple meal with people you love. In a journal, record your response to this experience. Is this something you can institute as a regular practice? What changes would you make going forward?

c. When we practice Sabbath rest, just as when we feast on God's presence in the midst of our troubles, we show others who are watching that God is good and that He is active in our lives. What are some other ways we can have an influence by fully embracing God's gifts to us and following His commands?

CHAPTER 7

WE INVITE JESUS TO TRANSFORM US

Jesus entered Jericho and made his way through the town. There was a man there named Zacchaeus. He was the chief tax collector in the region, and he had become very rich. He tried to get a look at Jesus, but he was too short to see over the crowd. So he ran ahead and climbed a sycamore-fig tree beside the road, for Jesus was going to pass that way.

When Jesus came by, he looked up at Zacchaeus and called him by name. "Zacchaeus!" he said. "Quick, come down! I must be a guest in your home today."

Zacchaeus quickly climbed down and took Jesus to his house in great excitement and joy. But the people were displeased. "He has gone to be the guest of a notorious sinner," they grumbled.

Meanwhile, Zacchaeus stood before the Lord and said, "I will give half my wealth to the poor, Lord, and if I have cheated people on their taxes, I will give them back four times as much!"

Jesus responded, "Salvation has come to this home today, for this man has shown himself to be a true son of Abraham. For the Son of Man came to seek and save those who are lost."

LUKE 19:1-10

Setting the Table

What a strange day it was in Jericho.

Dust cast a yellow haze upon the whole town as the crowd shuffled through the narrow streets, straining for a sight of the strange rabbi who had come to town. Why did such crowds follow this Jesus wherever He went? What was it they sought from Him? Perhaps some came limping, coughing, deaf, or blind, with the mustard seed of a hope that Jesus' hands really could heal them. Others must have come to hear the teaching of this man who spoke with authority. Still others made their way to the bustling road because they had nothing better to do—because they were bored, because they wanted to see what all the fuss was about.

Whatever the reasons held in the secret parts of each individual's heart, the town of Jericho was full to bursting that day. It was so full that Zacchaeus couldn't see over the heads of those who crowded around him.

What in the world was Zacchaeus doing there anyway? What could that corrupt old sinner want with the poor and passionate rabbi?

But he *was* there. As he made his way around the crowd, Zacchaeus was fixed with confused and irritated glances. The crowd knew this man as a wealthy tax collector and extorter of the poor. When Zacchaeus tried to squeeze through, they stopped him with cold and unmoving shoulders. Unable to see through the crowd, and not allowed to move through it, Zacchaeus made up his mind to climb a tree.

Peering down from his undignified perch, Zacchaeus finally spotted Jesus. And he could hardly believe it when he heard Jesus calling out to him.

"Quick, come down! I must be a guest in your home today."

This was a command, not a request, and to the surprise of everyone—perhaps including himself—Zacchaeus was happy to comply. The joy was evident on his face as he scrambled down the tree and led Jesus to his home.

The crowd followed, grumbling about Jesus' strange choice of dinner companion. They must have exchanged flabbergasted looks as Zacchaeus emerged later, clasping the hands of those he had extorted, promising to pay them back fourfold what he owed them.

What a strange day it was in Jericho when Zacchaeus was redeemed.

For many who grew up in the church, the story of Zacchaeus is strongly associated with a nauseatingly catchy song, complete with hand motions, about a "wee little man." The narrative has taken on a whimsical, almost humorous flair. How silly for a short, rich man to climb a tree to see Jesus! How nice that Jesus saves him. Someone bring out the animal crackers and apple juice.

This short passage, however, presents a much more epic theme: the invitation of Christ into a human heart and home and the transforming grace that extends from His presence. Zacchaeus is in many ways the prototypical sinner saved by grace. In these few verses, the reader witnesses the turning of a heart from greed, darkness, and lies to righteousness and active generosity. And all because Jesus asked to stay for lunch.

The first lesson that Zacchaeus teaches is that to receive Christ at our tables and in our hearts, we must humble ourselves. It took a tenacious humility for Zacchaeus to pursue Jesus the way he did. To climb a tree is not a dignified endeavor, especially for a man of elevated status, to whom many people are financially beholden. Zacchaeus's willingness to submit himself to such humiliation shows his level of dedication to finding Jesus.

A desire strong enough for Zacchaeus to humiliate himself in such a way must have been rooted in a deep knowledge of his own need for something outside of himself. This desire for Jesus and humble knowledge of our need must be at the root of our spiritual life as well.

The second truth that Zacchaeus's story reveals is that Jesus invites Himself into our lives in the midst of our mess and sin. There is something in Zacchaeus's story that seems backward: Jesus comes to Zacchaeus *before* Zacchaeus repents. This defies every altar call we have ever heard. The classic conversion story involves something of a narrative arc: repentance, conversion, transformation. But the story of Zacchaeus shows us that Jesus does not wait outside the door while we tidy up the corners of our lives. He invites Himself into our stickiest sins, where His loving presence causes repentance and renewal within us.

When we struggle to overcome a pattern of sin in our lives—sometimes struggling even to feel bad about it—we must remember the story of Zacchaeus and invite Jesus into our frustration and sin. Only His loving presence can move our hearts to true repentance.

Finally, this story shows us that Jesus' presence in our lives leads to radical transformation, moving us toward righteousness, generosity, and holiness. It is easy to sink into a definition of grace that allows us to live permissively, but Jesus' grace is one that enlivens our hearts and animates our good deeds. The arc of Zacchaeus's story makes it clear that this generous grace demands and produces a change in our lives. An experience of the infinite grace of Jesus naturally leads us to a different life, a sharing of the beauty we have tasted. His presence in our life should not make us presumptuous, but should call us instead to a deeper, richer, and more generous life.

The story of Zacchaeus is a surprising, backward story. But this should not surprise us. Jesus is the King of the upside-down Kingdom, where His love works in ways we don't expect and sometimes struggle to understand. Jesus doesn't invite Himself into the clean heart or wait until we tidy our souls and quit our addictions. Instead He invites Himself into the very midst of our sin and says, "Quick! I must be a guest in your home today!" We must only have the humility and the bravery to invite Him.

Table Talk

Conversation Starters

1. Describe a time when Jesus came to you or someone else in a way you totally didn't expect. What happened?

2. Do you think we always need to get to the point of desperation, willing to humiliate ourselves, before we let Jesus change us? Why or why not?

3. What aspect of your life do you tend to want to "clean up" before you invite Jesus (or anyone else) to come close and get to know you?

4. Have you ever struggled even to *want* to do the right thing? What happened?

Digging Deeper

1. *"The LORD is compassionate and merciful, slow to get angry and filled with unfailing love. He will not constantly accuse us, nor remain angry forever. He does not punish us for all our sins; he does not deal harshly with us, as we deserve. For his unfailing love toward those who fear him is as great as the height of the heavens above the earth. He has removed our sins as far from us as the east is from the west. The LORD is like a father to his children, tender and compassionate to those who fear him. For he knows how weak we are; he remembers we are only dust"* (PSALM 103:8-14).

a. When you struggle with sin, how do you usually imagine God's attitude toward you? Do you see Him as angry? Exasperated? Disappointed? Distant?

b. This passage reminds us that God understands our frailty and has compassion for us even in our sin and failures. When a toddler is exhausted and throws a tantrum or melts into tears, a parent usually isn't angry or surprised, but gentle and understanding. This is the picture of God that Psalm 103 paints for us. Read this passage through again. How does it affect your understanding of God? Does it change your attitude toward your own sin?

2. *"We know how much God loves us, and we have put our trust in his love. God is love, and all who live in love live in God, and God lives in them. And as we live in God, our love grows more perfect. So we will not be afraid on the day of judgment, but we can face him with confidence because we live like Jesus here in this world. Such love has no fear, because perfect love expels all fear. If we are afraid, it is for fear of punishment, and this shows that we have not fully experienced his perfect love. We love each other because he loved us first"* (1 JOHN 4:16-19).

a. This passage creates a sort of narrative about how we grow in love and righteousness. What is the order of that growth? What comes first, and what follows? Do you think the order can ever be reversed? Why or why not?

b. John says that "perfect love expels all fear" because "if we are afraid, it is for fear of punishment." Do you ever find yourself afraid of punishment? How does remembering that God's attitude toward you is love change your general outlook on life?

c. Our righteousness grows because we are firmly planted in God's initiating love toward us in the person of Jesus Christ. In order to grow, we must place our trust in His love. How do we do this? What does it mean for you to trust in God's love for you?

3. *"You love justice and hate evil. Therefore God, your God, has anointed you, pouring out the oil of joy on you more than on anyone else"* (Psalm 45:7).

   a. The psalmist speaks of righteousness not only as something we do, but as something we love. For a true transformation, the heart must be trained in this direction. How do you think this typically happens? Is it something we can do for ourselves?

   b. In light of the story of Zacchaeus and the Scriptures we have just studied, how do we develop these attitudes? (How was Zacchaeus's decision to treat his clients justly related to what happened with Jesus?)

CHAPTER 8

DUTY OR DELIGHT?

One of the Pharisees asked Jesus to have dinner with him, so Jesus went to his home and sat down to eat. When a certain immoral woman from that city heard he was eating there, she brought a beautiful alabaster jar filled with expensive perfume. Then she knelt behind him at his feet, weeping. Her tears fell on his feet, and she wiped them off with her hair. Then she kept kissing his feet and putting perfume on them.

When the Pharisee who had invited him saw this, he said to himself, "If this man were a prophet, he would know what kind of woman is touching him. She's a sinner!"

Then Jesus answered his thoughts. "Simon," he said to the Pharisee, "I have something to say to you."

"Go ahead, Teacher," Simon replied.

Then Jesus told him this story: "A man loaned money to two people—500 pieces of silver to one and 50 pieces to the other. But neither of them could repay him, so he kindly forgave them both, canceling their debts. Who do you suppose loved him more after that?"

Simon answered, "I suppose the one for whom he canceled the larger debt."

"That's right," Jesus said. Then he turned to the woman and said to Simon, "Look at this woman kneeling here. When I entered

your home, you didn't offer me water to wash the dust from my feet, but she has washed them with her tears and wiped them with her hair. You didn't greet me with a kiss, but from the time I first came in, she has not stopped kissing my feet. You neglected the courtesy of olive oil to anoint my head, but she has anointed my feet with rare perfume.

"I tell you, her sins—and they are many—have been forgiven, so she has shown me much love. But a person who is forgiven little shows only little love." Then Jesus said to the woman, "Your sins are forgiven."

The men at the table said among themselves, "Who is this man, that he goes around forgiving sins?"

And Jesus said to the woman, "Your faith has saved you; go in peace."

LUKE 7:36-50

Setting the Table

Simon the Pharisee opened the door to Jesus.

Why had Simon done this unorthodox thing? On one level, he was doing his duty. This itinerant rabbi had caused a great stir. He fascinated the people and threatened the status quo, causing annoyance and uneasiness among those in power. He must be investigated, and Simon was the man to do it. Being chosen to do this task was a point of some pride for him. He was to be trusted. He was in the club.

Fact finding. Nothing more.

And yet . . .

Simon was conscious of a niggling curiosity in his own mind. What was it about this man, that He held such sway over so many hearts? Tiptoeing through the shadowy corners of his mind, he wondered, *Could this man really be a prophet?*

And so Simon opened the door.

There was nothing marvelous about Jesus' appearance, no stateliness or majesty. He looked like a thousand other strangers you might pass on the street. Simon couldn't help but wonder what all the fuss was about.

Their eyes met, and there was a moment of awkward silence. Simon made a swift, definite movement with his head, and gestured for Jesus to come in.

As Jesus stepped into the hallway of the courtyard, the light from the doorway caught a cloud of a thousand dust particles floating in the air. Jesus' feet were caked in red dust from the streets, but Simon pretended not to notice. *Fact finding. That's what we're here for.*

He led Jesus to the dining area and with a brusque civility invited Him to recline at the table. Again Simon noted how unremarkable this man seemed, how unthreatening. And yet there was something in His unflappable manner that Simon found disarming.

Simon attempted to appear disinterested as the servants served the food. But all at once, a disturbance broke out.

There was a rush of movement and muffled voices, and then a woman appeared at the table. Her eyes were wild and urgent, and her uncovered hair fell in dark waves over her shoulders. In her hands she held a jar. Searching the room with purposeful intensity, her eyes fell on Jesus. Rushing over to Him, she knelt at His feet. She wept as if from joy and relief. As her tears fell, making little rivers in the dust on Jesus' feet, she wiped away the grime with her hair and gently kissed them again and again. From the jar she poured a pungent perfume whose fragrance wafted through the entire room.

Simon watched with a tinge of disgust. He recognized the woman. She was notorious for her indiscretions, the sort of person who could end your career simply by speaking to you on the street. *If Jesus were a prophet, He would know what kind of woman is touching him,* Simon thought.

"Simon," Jesus said, seeming to read his mind, "when I entered your home, you didn't offer Me water to wash the dust from My feet, but she has washed them with her tears and wiped them with her hair."

Jesus went on, telling some story about debtors, but Simon only half listened. Jesus had openly chided him for poor hospitality. *Unbelievable!* This man was truly a threat to Simon's way of life.

This is a passage about two hosts.

One is honorable, expected, and powerful. The other is dishonorable, suspect, and an invader. And yet Jesus proclaims that the so-called "immoral woman" is the more gracious host. In these two hosts we have models upon which to meditate, to consider how we host Jesus in our lives.

All through this story, it seems, we are witnessing acts

of hospitality. Jesus' own words help us understand this when He compares the actions of a woman who shows Jesus "much love" to the actions of a man who doesn't even bother to be polite.

Simon does only what is necessary when Jesus comes to visit. He does not tend to Jesus' physical needs nor care for Him as an individual. With wealth, status, and a home, it seems Simon would be a perfect host. But he doesn't even extend to Jesus the basics of hospitality as defined by his community—providing water for washing, greeting with a kiss.

The loving woman, on the other hand, attends to Jesus' needs. She washes His feet with her tears. She greets Him with tenderness and intimacy as she kisses His feet and rubs them with fragrant perfume.

In Simon's own home, he is outdone in hospitality.

It is significant that Jesus notes that Simon "neglected courtesy." To be courteous is to be polite, to show deference, and to tend to the needs of another before your own—ultimately to affirm the other person as an individual with value and dignity. It seems, then, that the "immoral woman" looks to Jesus as an individual worthy of courtesy and Simon the respectable Pharisee does not.

As we invite Jesus into our lives, are we courteous hosts? Do we greet Him in the morning in prayer? Do we attend to the dust on His feet, looking with care to see where He is moving in our lives? Do we anoint Him with praise?

Luke also directs our eyes to the differences in how Simon and the woman relate to Jesus. Simon's disposition is one of distanced investigation. He experiences a private incredulity at Jesus' treatment of the woman, but he never utters a word aloud regarding it. Simon embodies the skeptic and the cynic. Unwilling to risk even communication with Jesus, Simon refuses to express even his doubt.

It is easy to stay in the attitude of Simon. For whatever reason, we may invite Jesus into our lives. Perhaps we wish to test His truth; perhaps we wish to see what He's all about; perhaps it seems like the right thing to do. So we invite Him in, but we avoid making eye contact, as it were. We doubt Him in the privacy of our hearts but do not have the strength to say, "Lord, I believe; help my unbelief" (see Mark 9:24).

The woman who showed Jesus love teaches us a different way of hosting Him. Her relationship to Him is not tidy, expected, or smooth. But her gaze, her whole self, is turned toward Jesus to connect with Him, touch Him, relate to Him. In her we have a model. When we invite Christ into our lives and our hearts, we needn't be sure, have answers, cast out our doubts, or be perfect. But we must have our hearts turned toward Him. We cannot be healed if we hold the Healer at arm's distance.

The last—and crowning—difference Jesus notes between Simon and the woman is that of anointing. Jesus says, "You neglected the courtesy of olive oil to anoint My head, but she has anointed My feet with rare perfume."

The word *anointed* holds a special theological significance. In the Old Testament, anointing relates to holiness and to kingship. It is associated with the story of Samuel anointing David as the king of Israel. Our term *Christ*, in fact, comes from the Greek rendering of the word *Messiah*, meaning "anointed one." Jesus was born into a nation who awaited a messiah—an anointed king in the line of David who would come and put everything right.

When the woman anoints Jesus, she acknowledges His value, His holiness, and His kingship. Unlike those around her, she recognizes that He is the Messiah her people have been waiting for so long. Her actions culminate in a tender expression of worship. While Simon seems to hold his counsel regarding Jesus, the loving woman declares her allegiance, her love, and her thankfulness.

We daily have the opportunity to host Christ in our lives—through prayer in those moments before the force of day begins, through recognizing His presence in a piece of beautiful music that enlivens our hearts, through loving those around us who reflect God's image. But what sort of hosts will we be? Will we approach Him with courtesy, the deference shown for an individual we cherish, or will we treat Him as a question to be answered, a resource to be mined? Is our face turned toward Him and toward relationship, or do we maintain a distant, cynical stance? Do we invite Jesus in so that we may worship Him as the Messiah?

As we host Christ, may we find ourselves not in the position of Simon, standing at a distance from Jesus, tightly holding on to unspoken questions, but in the place of the woman who showed Jesus much love, worshiping Him because we know we are deeply loved and forgiven.

Table Talk

Conversation Starters

1. How do you think Simon saw himself on the day he invited Jesus over to his house? What were his motivations? What mattered most to him? And what do you think bothered him most about the events of that day?

2. What is the relationship between love and forgiveness in this story? Do you think that the so-called "immoral woman" already knew she was forgiven? Share any examples from your own life of forgiveness generating greater love.

3. In what ways do you think we avoid connecting with Jesus once we invite Him into our lives? How do we avoid Him?

4. In what ways can your thoughts and actions help anoint Jesus as King of your life?

Digging Deeper

1. *"What shall we say about such wonderful things as these? If God is for us, who can ever be against us? Since he did not spare even his own Son but gave him up for us all, won't he also give us everything else? Who dares accuse us whom God has chosen for his own? No one—for God himself has given us right standing with himself. Who then will condemn us? No one—for Christ Jesus died for us and was raised to life for us, and he is sitting in the place of honor at God's right hand,*

pleading for us. Can anything ever separate us from Christ's love? Does it mean he no longer loves us if we have trouble or calamity, or are persecuted, or hungry, or destitute, or in danger, or threatened with death? (As the Scriptures say, 'For your sake we are killed every day; we are being slaughtered like sheep.') No, despite all these things, overwhelming victory is ours through Christ, who loved us. And I am convinced that nothing can ever separate us from God's love. Neither death nor life, neither angels nor demons, neither our fears for today nor our worries about tomorrow—not even the powers of hell can separate us from God's love. No power in the sky above or in the earth below—indeed, nothing in all creation will ever be able to separate us from the love of God that is revealed in Christ Jesus our Lord" (ROMANS 8:31-39).

a. This passage describes God's overwhelming love for us and His forgiveness of our sins. Do you think that the woman who anointed Jesus' feet understood God's love for her? How would it change your way of hosting Jesus in your life if you knew deep in the corners of your heart that God loves you and will never let you go?

b. Imagine yourself as Simon the Pharisee. How would you respond if Jesus spoke the words of

Romans 8:31-39 to you? And now imagine yourself as the woman who was forgiven of her sins. Does the message—or how you receive it—change? What is your personal response to this message of God's steadfast love and forgiveness?

2. *"Shout with joy to the LORD, all the earth! Worship the LORD with gladness. Come before him, singing with joy. Acknowledge that the LORD is God! He made us, and we are his. We are his people, the sheep of his pasture. Enter his gates with thanksgiving; go into his courts with praise. Give thanks to him and praise his name. For the LORD is good. His unfailing love continues forever, and his faithfulness continues to each generation"* (PSALM 100).

   a. One of the key differences between Simon and the loving woman is that she came to worship Jesus, while Simon held Him at arm's distance. What do you think is the relationship between worship and forgiveness?

   b. What does worship mean to you? When do you feel most worshipful? When listening to beautiful music? When walking in creation? When enjoying

the company of people you love? In church? In your
room alone?

3. *"Keep your heart with all vigilance, for from it flow the
springs of life. Put away from you crooked speech, and
put devious talk far from you. Let your eyes look directly
forward, and your gaze be straight before you. Ponder the
path of your feet; then all your ways will be sure. Do not
swerve to the right or to the left; turn your foot away from
evil"* (PROVERBS 4:23-27, ESV).

    a. What comes out of your heart? When you are
walking in your day-to-day life, what have you made
the center of your will, the object of your desire? It
will direct you on one path or another, and not all
paths will lead to happiness and light. Every day
the choices you make with your heart will either
purify or poison the springs of life that come forth
from your heart. What choices will help you "keep
your heart" with vigilance and keep your "springs"
clear? What choices have the opposite effect? In your
personal life, what choices have you made that have
been either beneficial or damaging?

b. To walk forward in a straight line, we have to have perspective; we must cultivate a long-distance vision. If we don't keep looking toward our destination, we will be easily waylaid by the many voices and distractions that lie in wait all around us. In the Christian walk, what shapes our long-term vision? How can we hold on to an eternal perspective that keeps us on the right path?

c. In all likelihood, Simon the Pharisee whom Jesus visited was dedicated to keeping his heart pure and staying on the right path. He also probably assumed that the "immoral woman" had made all the wrong choices. To a point, he was probably right. So what was Simon missing? What truths did he fail to comprehend?

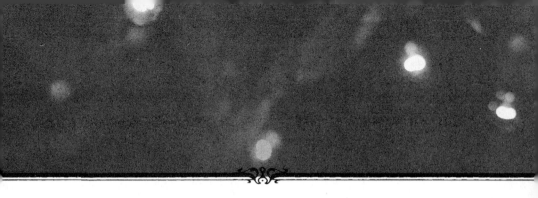

PART 3

We Prepare a Table for Others

CHAPTER 9

A FEAST IN THE PRESENCE OF ENEMIES

When Abigail saw David, she quickly got off her donkey and bowed low before him. She fell at his feet and said, "I accept all blame in this matter, my lord. Please listen to what I have to say. I know Nabal is a wicked and ill-tempered man; please don't pay any attention to him. He is a fool, just as his name suggests. But I never even saw the young men you sent. . . .

When the LORD has done all he promised and has made you leader of Israel, don't let this be a blemish on your record. Then your conscience won't have to bear the staggering burden of needless bloodshed and vengeance. And when the LORD has done these great things for you, please remember me, your servant!"

David replied to Abigail, "Praise the LORD, the God of Israel, who has sent you to meet me today! Thank God for your good sense! Bless you for keeping me from murder and from carrying out vengeance with my own hands. For I swear by the LORD, the God of Israel, who has kept me from hurting you, that if you had not hurried out to meet me, not one of Nabal's men would still be alive tomorrow morning." Then David accepted her present and told her, "Return home in peace. I have heard what you said. We will not kill your husband."

1 SAMUEL 25:23-25, 30-35

Setting the Table

David was livid. The heat was rising to his head, and he could feel the pulsing anger pounding out its furious rhythm. He knew he wasn't a particularly patient man, but he sought to be a just man who treated others with parity and fair-mindedness. And although he was the anointed king, he had waited long and made no move to usurp the throne of the current king, Saul.

These days his life seemed to be perpetually in flux— sometimes in an uneasy peace with Saul and sometimes on the run for his life. Because of this, he understood what it felt like to be at others' mercy. And when ordinary folk stumbled upon his encampment, he understood how easy it would be for such people to see his mighty warriors as a threat, agitators ready to cause harm. Consequently, he made extensive efforts to show his men's peacefulness and their rightful actions in regard to the stranger.

The shepherds from near Carmel who had stayed in their encampment were just such people. When they first arrived, David had seen the distrust in their faces; clearly, they'd felt exposed to potential harm. So David had made it clear to his men that these shepherds were to be treated with the utmost kindness and generosity. His soldiers were not to steal from, harass, or otherwise trouble the visitors in their midst.

David knew his good treatment of the shepherds would be his calling card all around Israel. His standing in the kingdom was uncertain—many distrusted him, though others saw him as the proper solution to the problem of Saul. So his reputation as a man of character was of immense importance to his and his company's survival in the land.

It had now been some time since the shepherds had stayed in David's stronghold. They had departed in peace, some as friends. David had been very pleased with the way things developed and had felt certain that his acts of goodwill would earn dividends if he were to encounter the group again. So when he found himself in Carmel—during sheepshearing time, no less—his mind quickly turned to his positive encounter with the shepherds. He remembered the name of their master, Nabal, whom he had not met, but who surely would receive David as a friend.

David quickly sent emissaries to seek out Nabal and request shelter and food. Then he waited in patience, looking forward to enjoying company with Nabal's shepherds during their most celebratory event of the year, the shearing of all their sheep. But when the response came back, his smile quickly faded. Nabal had called him a runaway and his fellow soldiers a "band of outlaws."

David's temper immediately turned him toward his sword, his old ally during times of rage. He wouldn't take on King Saul until such a time as God Himself ordained, but he would have no problem blotting out this scourge of a man Nabal from the face of the earth. The man surely deserved it; there had to be retribution for such an insult, especially after all the kindness David had shown to Nabal's servants.

David grew more and more enraged as he and his men

put on armor and took up their weapons. Who was this little gnat of a man to challenge him? "A lot of good it did to help this fellow," he raged. "He has repaid me evil for good."

As he drew close to Nabal's property, David fully expected to see armed men coming out to meet them in combat. *Good,* he thought. *Let them come.* He turned to his men and rashly declared, "May God strike me and kill me if even one man of his household is still alive tomorrow morning!"

Soon he did indeed see a cavalcade of people coming from the direction of Nabal's house. But instead of clinking armor and shining spears, sweet aromas gently reached his senses. Whiffs of fig and roasted lamb arrested his fury in its place, and he was momentarily confused. Who comes out to fight with delicacies fit for a king? That would be impractical, wasteful. This was a strange people indeed.

As the group drew closer, David could see that whole baskets of bread, raisins, and other treats were loaded onto the backs of donkeys. He furrowed his brow. What was the meaning of this? This wasn't a war party; it was a moving feast. The donkeys carried food far beyond the needs of the meager collection of people coming their way.

As the two bands drew close to each other, they both stopped. Out of the ranks of servants completely unprepared for war emerged a beautiful woman. Her bearing and clothing identified her as the lady of the house. She carried with her a basket of delectable morsels whose enticing fragrance enveloped David and caused him to sway, ever so slightly, in his rage. He would not hold off on the coming slaughter of this recalcitrant household, but perhaps he would listen to this woman for a moment and hear what nonsense she would have to say after Nabal's treachery.

But the woman did more than talk. She laid aside her basket of fig cakes, fell at David's feet, and pleaded with him miserably. Her husband was a fool, she said, and had she been able to speak with the men from David's camp, she would have given them the courtesy and greeting they deserved. David was still unamused, but he reached down and took a fig cake. A delicious warmth spread all over him as he held it to his nose and breathed in the heady aroma. He took a bite, and the taste cast him into unexpected throes of delight.

The woman continued. To David's surprise, she laid the blame of the whole affair on herself and asked for his mercy. She lavished him with praise, proclaiming that he was "fighting the Lord's battles."

David did not think of himself as an easily flattered man or one susceptible to such blatant bribery. But somewhere between the flaky crust of the fig cake he had just finished off and the excellent vintage of wine which he was now enthusiastically consuming, he gradually began cooling off. Perhaps he had been too hasty. Certainly the carnage of battle could wait until he finished the succulent piece of lamb a servant had just handed him.

He continued to hear the woman's pleas and was surprised to find himself losing the conviction of his indignation. By the time the woman completed her monologue, he was completely mollified, and as he thought of what to say in response, he felt uncomfortably close to feeling ashamed at his rash behavior.

"Thank God for your good sense!" he said. "Bless you for keeping me from murder and from carrying out vengeance with my own hands. For I swear by the Lord, the God of Israel, who has kept me from hurting you, that if you had not hurried out to meet me, not one of Nabal's men would still be alive tomorrow morning. Return home in peace. I have heard what you said. We will not kill your husband."

In reality, neither Nabal nor David was a particularly judicious or even-minded man. David could be just as unjust and reckless as the foe he intended to destroy. Abigail, wise as she was, knew it would take more than simple pleading to assuage David's wrath. So she used food and words of peace to win him over.

It is easy to think of food as something we share with those who are at peace with us, those whom we like and who like us in return. But what about sharing food with our enemies? Sharing a meal or treat with people who dislike us or mean us harm is a way to show them that we are people of peace. As Christians, we give of our very resources to all because God has called us to forgiveness and kindness and gives Himself in fullness to exemplify what that looks like.

It is "the kindness of God" that "leads [people] to repentance" (Romans 2:4, NASB). And as bearers of Christ's presence into the world, we are called to show the kindness that will lead others to repentance in Jesus' name. When we share a meal with those who seem far from us, we are walking not only in the footsteps of wise Abigail, but also in the way of Jesus Himself.

Today, as you think about people who are difficult for you to like, who cause you to feel hurt or who seem like unsolvable problems, consider preparing a table to bless them with the kindness of the Lord. Perhaps you will be surprised at how God uses the very real grace of food and drink to change minds and hearts.

Table Talk

CONVERSATION STARTERS

1. Abigail's actions have often been applauded as wise and judicious. Is there anything about her actions that bothers you? Does she seem manipulative or simply fearful? What is the difference between appeasing an enemy and reaching out to him or her in dignity and kindness?

2. Have you ever had success in winning over a problem person in your life with the gift of food or a meal? What happened?

3. Why do you think food is such a powerful tool in mending relationships and keeping the peace? Practically speaking, how would you go about sharing food with an enemy or difficult person? (Invite him to lunch? Bake her some cookies?)

4. Do you think that sharing food with our enemies or the difficult people in our lives is always helpful or a good idea? What makes the difference? What is the alternative?

DIGGING DEEPER

1. *"A gentle answer deflects anger, but harsh words make tempers flare"* (PROVERBS 15:1).

   a. What kinds of situations tend to make you angry and tempt you to respond with harsh words? What can help you respond gently or positively instead? Do you think there is ever a place for a strong or negative response to an affront or offense? Why or why not?

   b. Think of someone in your life who is difficult— perhaps a child who has an attitude, a colleague who is chronically irritating, or a friend who has offended you. Write down a couple of kind sentences that you can keep in your mind to speak to that person when you see him or her next (no matter what they may say to you).

2. *"If your enemies are hungry, feed them. If they are thirsty, give them something to drink. In doing this, you will heap burning coals of shame on their heads"* (ROMANS 12:20).

    a. Do you think the apostle Paul is saying that we should treat our enemies kindly in order to hurt them? If not, what is the real point of this verse? How can it help you respond to those who treat you poorly?

    b. What is a practical way you can bless those who seem opposed to you? In keeping with the spirit of Abigail, a meal or treat served in kindness is a good start, but perhaps there are other ways that are a more natural fit with your life and talents. List three things that you might do to bless another person, even someone you see as an enemy or antagonist.

3. *"Bless those who persecute you. Don't curse them; pray that God will bless them"* (ROMANS 12:14).

    a. It is so easy to say to the Lord, "I will be gracious when this person repents and comes back around to walking in goodness." But the Bible specifically calls us to bless people when they are in the midst of their sin, even when they are treating us with animosity. Make a private list of those people in your life, people you resent and might have withheld God's blessing from. What would it take for you to be able to honestly bless those people rather than curse them (out loud or in your mind)?

b. One way to become a person who blesses others, no matter how they have treated you, is to go from being reactive to being proactive—thinking ahead about your feelings and reactions to a person or circumstance and how you will respond in the future. Using journalism's famous "five Ws" can help you do this. To practice, choose a recent situation that has bothered you and answer the following questions:

- *Who* do you feel has been unkind to you?

- *Why* in particular do you feel mistreated?

- *When* did the mistreatment happen? (Is there a long-running grief that underpins your interaction with certain people, or are you habitually inclined to react to them in the moment because of their personality or immaturity?)

- *Where* did you have a reactive reaction? (What environments are particularly tricky for you?)

- *What* do you intend to do to change your pattern of reaction? (How will you speak and act?)

When you become a proactive person, you can enter any conversation with a blessing ready on your lips, having already prepared for the chance that they may not respond in kind. You will still be able to bless because God is your great blessing and His blessing overflows in your life.

CHAPTER 10

A TABLE OF ANTICIPATION

The LORD said to Elijah, "Go and live in the village of Zarephath, near the city of Sidon. I have instructed a widow there to feed you."

So he went to Zarephath. As he arrived at the gates of the village, he saw a widow gathering sticks, and he asked her, "Would you please bring me a little water in a cup?" As she was going to get it, he called to her, "Bring me a bite of bread, too."

But she said, "I swear by the LORD your God that I don't have a single piece of bread in the house. And I have only a handful of flour left in the jar and a little cooking oil in the bottom of the jug. I was just gathering a few sticks to cook this last meal, and then my son and I will die."

But Elijah said to her, "Don't be afraid! Go ahead and do just what you've said, but make a little bread for me first. Then use what's left to prepare a meal for yourself and your son. For this is what the LORD, the God of Israel, says: There will always be flour and olive oil left in your containers until the time when the LORD sends rain and the crops grow again!"

So she did as Elijah said, and she and Elijah and her family continued to eat for many days.

1 KINGS 17:8-15

Setting the Table

She could not remember the last time it had rained.

This realization came to her as she walked outside to fetch sticks for the fire. Was it last summer? Or the summer before that? Kindling was so easy to find these days because every branch in the thicket was bone dry.

She made a good deal of noise as she snapped off branches and was thus surprised when she turned to see someone standing behind her.

He was a wild-looking man. His hair was a tangled halo, and he looked to have lived in the unsheltered sun.

"Would you please bring me a little water in a cup?" he said.

She nodded and turned toward the well to retrieve it. As she walked, she wondered if he was one of the few who had refused to worship the idols brought in by King Ahab's wife, Jezebel. Was he the one who had predicted this terrible drought?

"Bring me a bite of bread, too."

Her stomach dropped. Her circumstances were bad enough. Did she have to admit them to a stranger? She steeled herself to speak matter-of-factly.

"I swear by the Lord your God that I don't have a single piece of bread in the house. And I have only a handful of flour left in the jar and a little cooking oil in the bottom of the jug. I was just gathering a few sticks to cook this last meal. And then my son and I will die."

She found herself shaking as she finished. Speaking the words out loud made it all real. She had run out of resources and was preparing to meet death. That was all there was to it.

"Do not be afraid," the man said with a sudden and stern tenderness. "Go ahead and do as you have said, just bring me a little bread first. For the Lord of Israel says that your jar and your jug will be full until He sends rain upon the crops."

She didn't even have the energy to question him. She simply turned and walked into her tiny house, reaching for her depleted containers of flour and oil. What, after all, did she have to lose?

Pouring the olive oil in the bowl, she watched as little ponds of it collected in the flour, the sight dissolving into memories of walks near the full river with her husband and infant son, of her world before drought and death and loss. She folded the oil in with the flour, and the memory disappeared into bleak reality.

It was only her and her son now. And the prophet, who had asked such an audacious favor and promised such an unbelievable miracle.

She closed her eyes for an instant, intentionally pushing back despair. Yes, she had lost a great deal, but so had everyone else. And she had been given so much as well. She had been married, and she had a child, her gift of all gifts. With her husband gone, this child had been her hope. She had always taken him as a sign from God that she was not forgotten. She had cherished him and had made a life using what she did have. But now even that little bit was almost gone. The two of them were in God's hands now.

All we can do in life is to faithfully use what has been given to us. She told herself this as she kneaded her small loaf. *Be thankful for what you are given, shape it as faithfully as you can, and when the ingredients of your life run out, accept it with grace and bravery.*

This was all she knew to do.

And so she made the prophet some bread.

There are times when we feel that we have no more to give, that our jar is empty. Financially we cannot bear the burden of having another family over for dinner. Physically, we are exhausted from another day of chasing little feet around the house, giving all of our strength to kisses, and giggles, and tedious discipline. Emotionally, we are too drained to cope with all the complicated mess of relating to other humans— the hurt feelings, broken hearts, and hot tempers. Spiritually, we feel our own doubts and questions too keenly to answer the questions of another. In our hearts we may want to be generous, kind, lifegiving, but we just don't have it in us.

We find ourselves, like the widow with Elijah, saying, "I swear by the Lord your God that I don't have a single piece of bread—or patience, or energy, or inspiration—left."

These moments are not a sign of failure. They are a sign of humanity. As this book has hopefully demonstrated, God created us as dependent beings with needs and does not despise us for those needs.

Only verses before this chapter's story, God ministered to the depleted and depressed Elijah through food and gentle care (see 1 Kings 17:2-6). But the story of the widow raises a different question for us: How can we—or ought we—set a table for others when we feel we have nothing to offer?

We are not called to set a table only when it is easy or when we feel we have extra left over. Sometimes God's greatest work and kindness is shown when we give out of what we *don't* have—that is, when we give in faith. The widow in this story, with her bleak realism and stark faith, presents to us a beautiful model of this. To set our table in faith, even when we don't feel like we have enough, reflects an attitude that receives life as a gift, that allows us to be fed by God through feeding others and to learn the power of simple generosity.

In our modern world, we often live under an illusion of control. We push buttons and make things happen. We learn to be assertive and proactive, to take charge when things go wrong and do whatever is necessary to make them go right. We grow accustomed to thinking we have at least cursory control over most things, with the possible exception of the weather and other people—and wouldn't mind taking a stab at those things too if we could.

In this control-oriented world, it is so easy to forget that at the heart of it, life is a gift. Each breath we take involves a complex intermingling of bodily systems that we do nothing to consciously sustain. Each day, sunny or gloomy, good or bad, is something we do not create, but can only receive.

It is sometimes easier to understand this reality when some of the things we count on are taken away. Perhaps an asthmatic better understands the miracle of breath, or a refugee better understands the benefit of having a home. Even just a moment of imagining our lives without a home, health, or loved ones reveals the fragility of the gift of life.

When we learn to consciously accept life as a gift, we can begin to live in the economy of grace. This means that we set our tables not out of obligation, guilt, or misplaced optimism, but in acknowledgment of God's provision. We are prepared to give, even in our poverty, because of our acute awareness that everything we possess comes from God. We are not in control of our daily circumstances—He is.

Living in a time and place where lack of control of life was a daily reality, the widow displayed a profound understanding of life as a gift. She acknowledged, quite plainly, the limitations of her possessions, but this did not stop her from deciding to give what little she had as an act of faith. This was a simple generosity; she did not prepare a lavish feast, but her gift was generous nonetheless. She gave out of what she had, acknowledging it as a gift and trusting, it seems, in God's provision.

When she did that, she learned firsthand the second benefit of setting a table in faith: It is often when we feed others that God feeds us. Through the widow's decision to give to Elijah even out of her need and lack, her own family was provided for. As she acted as a host to Elijah, God acted as a host to her. This reflects a profound spiritual truth: When we set a table for others—both spiritually and literally—in the place of our need, we experience God's grace and provision for us.

In a fallen world, it is only natural that sometimes we will become depleted. When we find ourselves saying to God, "My jar is empty. I have nothing more to give," we must remember that God knows and deeply cares about our needs. But in our moments of lack, we have an opportunity to turn our faces up, to remember that life and all our resources are gifts, to give in faith, and to be fed as we feed others. It is in these acts of weary faith that so often we meet God most intimately and He provides for us most richly.

Table Talk

CONVERSATION STARTERS

1. Describe a time in your life when you felt more was being asked of you than you were able to give. How did you respond? What happened?

2. Why do you think most of us cling so tightly to the belief that we're in control of our lives?

3. What are some practical examples of giving out of our need (at the table and otherwise)?

4. Do you think that most of us have to come to the end of our personal resources before we truly understand God's economy of grace? Why or why not?

1. *"Faith shows the reality of what we hope for; it is the evidence of things we cannot see. Through their faith, the people in days of old earned a good reputation. . . . All these people died still believing what God had promised them. They did not receive what was promised, but they saw it all from a distance and welcomed it. They agreed that they were foreigners and nomads here on earth. Obviously people who say such things are looking forward to a country they can call their own. If they had longed for the country they came from, they could have gone back. But they were looking for a better place, a heavenly homeland. That is why God is not ashamed to be called their God, for he has prepared a city for them"* (HEBREWS 11:1-2, 13-16).

   a. Hebrews 11 is famously called the Hall of Faith because it describes all the people in the Bible who lived "by faith." After reading this passage, what do you think it means to live by faith? Is there a particular area in your current life where you think God may be calling you now to live by faith? What would that look like?

   b. What do you think it means to live for something you can only "see in the distance"? Do you find it easy to live with this sort of vision, or is it easier for you to get caught up in the moment? What steps could you take to build your faith by sharpening your vision?

2. *"While Jesus was in the Temple, he watched the rich people dropping their gifts in the collection box. Then a poor widow came by and dropped in two small coins. 'I tell you the truth,' Jesus said, 'this poor widow has given more than all the rest of them. For they have given a tiny part of their surplus, but she, poor as she is, has given everything she has'"* (LUKE 21:1-4).

   a. What aspect of the widow's gift did Jesus find meaningful? How is God's economy of worth different from what makes things worthwhile in our world?

   b. It is easy to give when we have enough, but much more difficult when we have little. What do you find to be most difficult about giving out of faith? How can seeing life as a gift change this difficulty?

3. *"Give freely and become more wealthy; be stingy and lose everything. The generous will prosper; those who refresh others will themselves be refreshed"* (PROVERBS 11:24-25).

   a. Do you agree with this proverb? Have you ever known someone who was generous in the way this verse describes? What was he or she like? What kind of wealth do you think the verse is describing?

   b. What do you think it means that "those who refresh others will themselves be refreshed"? What causes the refreshing in our lives—our actions or God's blessing on us? What if God has designed us so that it is both?

CHAPTER 11

FOOD FOR THE UNFED

As Jesus was walking along, he saw a man named Matthew sitting at his tax collector's booth. "Follow me and be my disciple," Jesus said to him. So Matthew got up and followed him.

Later, Matthew invited Jesus and his disciples to his home as dinner guests, along with many tax collectors and other disreputable sinners. But when the Pharisees saw this, they asked his disciples, "Why does your teacher eat with such scum?"

When Jesus heard this, he said, "Healthy people don't need a doctor—sick people do." Then he added, "Now go and learn the meaning of this Scripture: 'I want you to show mercy, not offer sacrifices.' For I have come to call not those who think they are righteous, but those who know they are sinners."

MATTHEW 9:9-13

Setting the Table

Imagine that Jesus appeared today and had a dinner party. Who do you think He would invite?

Do you immediately start making a mental list of the best, godliest people you know? Perhaps Jesus would invite those of influence, those who make big decisions. Or perhaps He would look for the best, the smartest, the most creative.

Do you wonder if He would invite you?

I wonder if the Jews of Jesus' day imagined a similar scenario. As they awaited the promised Messiah, the one they thought would liberate their people, perhaps they dreamed that they would be good and wise enough to sit at the Messiah's table. Perhaps the Pharisees cherished a secret (or not-so-secret) hope that when the Messiah came, they would be important, pure, and wise enough to dine with the coming Savior of Israel.

But of course we needn't imagine what sort of people Jesus would invite. We know. Indeed, Jesus' dining companions were so well known to everyone that He was called "a glutton and a drunkard, and a friend of tax collectors and other sinners!" (Matthew 11:19). Jesus' tendency to eat and drink with the outcasts of society was not an occasional quirk, but a regular habit. He shared His table with the sick, the ceremonially unclean, the sinful, the disliked, the dishonest. What a surprise it must have been to some to see Him surrounded by the questionable and the outcasts. And what a disappointment it must have been to others. What kind of Messiah would do that?

In first-century Judaism, Jesus' table behavior was not only odd, but completely unacceptable. At that time, to share your table with someone was to associate yourself with his or her beliefs and ways of life. Dining with a wise teacher would somehow impart their wisdom to your reputation. To eat with the righteous was to be seen as righteous yourself, but to eat with a sinner was to take that person's soiled reputation onto yourself. And so the righteous, the clean, the well, and the wise ate together, politely rejecting those who might stain their reputation. The unbelieving, the sinners, and the sick were left to peer in from the outside or find their own table.

It is no wonder that the Pharisees were offended by Jesus' choice of dinner-table companions.

I wonder if perhaps our tables do not look so different from those of the Pharisees. Do we surround ourselves with those who are clean, orderly, righteous, and similar to us? Are we afraid of what people might think of us if we had *that* person to dinner? Are people surprised by how hospitable we are to those who are different from us—even those that others might disapprove of?

Hospitality to all is the way of Jesus. Jesus invited all to His table—the sinners, the sick, even the Pharisees. While the first-century religious elite saw the table as a place where sin was contagious, Jesus made the table the place where goodness was contagious. Through eating at the same table as those who were deemed unacceptable, He took on their sin by association. Rather than waiting for the clean, good, kind, and healthy to join His table, Jesus invited all so that they might taste and see His goodness. From this place of spiritual hospitality, Jesus discipled and instructed. People listened and were changed because they had experienced the richness and beauty of Jesus' grace.

Victor Hugo's great classic novel *Les Misérables* contains an example of just such generosity. A humble bishop invites a convict named Jean Valjean into his home for dinner and treats him as a member of the family. He doesn't even inquire about Valjean's background, but insists, "This is not my house; it is the house of Jesus Christ."[3]

Even after this kindness, Valjean steals the bishop's silver candlesticks and makes off into the night. He is quickly apprehended by the police. But rather than condemn him to jail again, the bishop testifies that he *gave* Valjean the candlesticks. With this gift the bishop tells Valjean that he has bought Valjean's soul for God and encourages him to live a righteous life. The generosity Jean Valjean experiences at the home of the bishop transforms his life and trickles into the lives of all the individuals he engages with afterward.

What a powerful message those words of the bishop convey: "This is not my house; it is the house of Jesus Christ." They paint a picture of what each Christian table ought to be like—always open to the unusual, the unlucky, and the unloved because Christ's table is open to all.

And we are invited to Jesus' table as well! Jesus' life shows us that wholeness and belief come only from an encounter with Christ, which means we must all come to the table before we can be redeemed. I think we sometimes forget this essential truth. Before we invite anyone to our table, we must remember that Christ has invited us to His. He has accepted us in our inadequate, weary, sinful state. He has washed us and made a place at the table for us to dine with Him. We are all sinners at Jesus' table, receiving His generous love.

It is easy to read the story of Jesus' life and conclude, "Ah, yes. I, too, should invite the sinner to my table." And this is a proper conclusion—as far as it goes. But we should never forget that every Christian is the sinner that Christ invites to the table. We all struggle, fail, and fall short again and again, but Christ still invites us all to the table. As we feed at His table, we find that there is more than enough for us, so our own generosity is the necessary, required response. In our lives, we can be both Valjean and the bishop.

A life with Jesus is one that illuminates everything with meaning—and that's true of the lifegiving table as well. His love radiates from the warmth of freshly baked bread. His joy shines in the sparkling eyes of loved ones around the table. His welcome flickers in the candlelight and floats on every aromatic current of air. With every meal we share, we're invited to feed on the generosity, grace, and joy of Jesus, and to let it illuminate our table with delight. And in the spirit of the Host of the feast, it follows naturally that we invite others to taste and see that the Lord is good.

The hospitality we offer others is an extension of the hospitality we experience from Jesus. To feed someone at your table is to affirm their value. It is something freely offered, without an agenda, with no attempt to convince or change them. However, I have often found that such hospitality can become the entryway to deeper conversations. Having a conversation about Jesus with someone for the first time can feel awkward, but inviting someone to a Christmas party or a family dinner reduces that tension. When people experience God's love for them through genuine kindness, true acceptance, and delicious food, their hearts are far more likely to open—and be ready to meet the One who has made a table for all of us.

Table Talk

Conversation Starters

1. Just for fun, imagine that you are holding a dinner party for Jesus and eight other people. Who would you invite? Why?

2. How would your mealtimes change if you thought of your own home as "the house of Jesus Christ"?

3. What barriers—practical or emotional—prevent you from initiating hospitality more often?

4. Name at least three changes you could make that would help you get past those barriers.

Digging Deeper

1. *"And it happened that [Jesus] was reclining at the table . . . and many tax collectors and sinners were dining with Jesus and His disciples; for there were many of them. . . . When the scribes of the Pharisees saw that He was eating with the sinners and tax collectors, they said to His disciples, 'Why is He eating and drinking with tax collectors and sinners?' And hearing this, Jesus said to them, 'It is not those who are healthy who need a physician, but those who are sick; I did not come to call the righteous, but sinners'"* (MARK 2:15-17, NASB).

    a. Who do you think would be the twenty-first-century equivalent of "sinners and tax collectors"? How would you perceive someone who had these people to dinner in their home? Would you go if you were invited?

b. How would you sum up Jesus' attitude toward nonbelievers from these passages? How do you engage with the non-Christians in your life? Do you seek out nonbelievers, or do you surround yourself with people who are like you? Do you stick up for the nonbelievers in your life like Jesus stuck up for those in His life? How might you initiate friendships with more people who are different from you?

2. *"I thank Christ Jesus our Lord, who has given me strength to do his work. He considered me trustworthy and appointed me to serve him, even though I used to blaspheme the name of Christ. In my insolence, I persecuted his people. But God had mercy on me because I did it in ignorance and unbelief. Oh, how generous and gracious our Lord was! He filled me with the faith and love that come from Christ Jesus. This is a trustworthy*

saying, and everyone should accept it: 'Christ Jesus came into the world to save sinners'—and I am the worst of them all. But God had mercy on me so that Christ Jesus could use me as a prime example of his great patience with even the worst sinners. Then others will realize that they, too, can believe in him and receive eternal life. All honor and glory to God forever and ever! He is the eternal King, the unseen one who never dies; he alone is God. Amen" (1 TIMOTHY 1:12-17).

a. Do you think the apostle Paul would have been the sort to sit around Jesus' table? It is easy to think that Jesus was against the Pharisees, but this can't be the case because Paul, one of the great early Christians, was a Pharisee. Why do you think Paul, a Pharisee, was different from some of the hard-hearted Pharisees?

b. Paul looks on his sinful past without shame, knowing that God has redeemed it and uses even his mistakes to bring others to the Lord. How do you look on your past mistakes? Are you able to have the same sort of vision for God's work in your life, or do you shy away from your past in shame? How does it change your perspective to know that Jesus invites you to His table no matter what?

3. *"A man had two sons. The younger son told his father, 'I want my share of your estate now before you die.' So his father agreed to divide his wealth between his sons. A few days later this younger son packed all his belongings and moved to a distant land, and there he wasted all his money in wild living. . . . When he finally came to his senses, he said to himself, 'At home even the hired servants have food enough to spare, and here I am dying of hunger! I will go home to my father and say, "Father, I have sinned against both heaven and you, and I am no longer worthy of being called your son. Please take me on as a hired servant."' So he returned home to his father. And while he was still a long way off, his father saw him coming. Filled with love and compassion, he ran to his son, embraced him, and kissed him. His son said to him, 'Father, I have sinned against both heaven and you, and I am no longer worthy of being called your son.' But his father said to the servants, 'Quick! Bring the finest robe in the house and put it on him. Get a ring for his finger and sandals for his feet. And kill the calf we have been fattening. We must celebrate with a feast, for this son of mine was dead and has now returned to life. He was lost, but now he is found.' So the party began"* (LUKE 15:11-13, 17-24).

a. Here we see Jesus' story about a good father throwing a huge feast for his disgraced and sinful son. How do you think this story interacts with Jesus' attitude toward feasting with outsiders? What further insight does it give us?

b. What is God's heart toward those who are currently living without knowing Him? How does this story reveal that? How does this shape the way you love and live with your non-Christian friends?

c. The father in this story causes everyone to stare and wonder as he welcomes back his profligate son. Are we equally willing to show generosity and celebration for those who return to or discover the faith? How could we celebrate with those who choose to follow Jesus with lives unlike our own?

CHAPTER 12

UNITED BY GOD'S PROVISION

All the believers were united in heart and mind. And they felt that what they owned was not their own, so they shared everything they had. The apostles testified powerfully to the resurrection of the Lord Jesus, and God's great blessing was upon them all. There were no needy people among them, because those who owned land or houses would sell them and bring the money to the apostles to give to those in need.

ACTS 4:32-35

Setting the Table

"All the believers were united in heart and mind." In the beginning days of the church, this was an undeniable truth. In fellowship with each other, sharing together in Christ's Spirit, the body of Christ acted as a whole, spreading the good news of Jesus' resurrection. Jesus Himself had prayed for that very reality: "I am praying not only for these disciples but also for all who will ever believe in me through their message . . . that they will all be one" (John 17:20-21).

The earliest Christians understood this not just in spirit, but also in their day-to-day lives. What was believed and shared as a spiritual practice needed to become a practical reality in the life of the church, and to this end the earliest Christians gave abundantly. Scripture tells us that "they felt that what they owned was not their own, so they shared everything they had." Because of this generous, self-giving hospitality, "there were no needy people among them." Jesus' resurrection had shown them that God's power was strong to save. So they held everything they had loosely for the sake of the Kingdom, confident that God would provide for all their needs.

But as with all great movements, not everything went according to plan. Some, like Ananias and his wife, Sapphira, did not appreciate the saving provision of God's Spirit. They thought to keep a bit behind just as a contingency plan and then conceal it from the apostles, as if the Lord Himself was in the dark to their deception (Acts 5:1-10). In other areas of the church, arguments arose, and people began to form into factions following Apollos or Paul or other leaders who seemed to represent the practices and theology that most suited them.

Jesus had surely understood what would come to pass in those fledgling moments of the church. Unity was His desire from the beginning—that His people would show their love for Him by seeking peace and reconciliation with each other. With that in mind, Jesus used the final few hours of His life to establish a special ritual that would cement the vital beauty of unity in the mind of each Christian.

He instituted a meal.

You see, a meal has the capacity to heal divisions, to draw disparate people and groups toward each other. At the table, people must choose to leave behind both the privilege they feel they deserve and, on the inverse, their fear of not being accepted, for it is the host of a table who invites each guest to attend and who gives each one honor by blessing them with nourishment. At the table, all sit side by side without regard to background, social status, ethnicity, or other differentiation. And all enjoy the same meal, choosing to honor their host, who has drawn each guest to the table because of His favor for them. Jesus is the Host of His meal—what we now call Communion, the Lord's Supper, or the Eucharist—and anyone who eats at His table is called to give up all presuppositions about anyone else who may join in as well.

Jesus imbued His Communion table with unifying power. Sadly, that power has often been abused, used instead as a means of exclusion and division. Leaders in the early church recognized this potential failure of practice and in some instances even had to step in to correct it. In 1 Corinthians 11, Paul firmly reprimanded those who saw the table as a place for their own gratification, who took Christ's gift and used it for their own ends while others went hungry. Paul knew this was antithetical to what Jesus had intended for the participatory and potent practice of the Communion meal.

Jesus instituted His holy meal to encourage humility; not as a privilege that some would be able to hold over others, but as a gift that all could gratefully receive from the true, generous Giver. Spoken on that fateful evening before He was betrayed, and repeated in the Communion meal every time it is taken by Christians as a corporate body, the sacred words ring true: "This is my body, which is given for you. Do this to remember me. . . . This cup is the new covenant between God and his people—an agreement confirmed with my blood, which is poured out as a sacrifice for you" (Luke 22:19-20). The Communion meal reminds us every time we partake of it that Christ gave everything for us and held nothing back, not even His own life.

When we take the bread, we are admonished to "remember." And when we recall Jesus' bodily sacrifice, we know there is nothing Jesus asks us to give up that He hasn't first laid down at the feet of His heavenly Father. How can we give anything less? No matter how much we give, we will always have the fullness of Christ within us, and that is a possession that can never be taken away.

And when we take the "cup of salvation" (Psalm 116:13), we are called to be like those who have given up "every weight that slows us down" (Hebrews 12:1)—to proclaim the new covenant between God and us as a unified people, no longer held back and cordoned off by either our own prejudices or our fears of rejection. As Paul reminds the Galatians, "There is no longer Jew or Gentile, slave or free, male and female. For you are all one in Christ Jesus" (3:28).

Whenever we provide a meal for others, we have the chance to extend that Communion power to those around us, to achieve the same unity that was so important to Jesus and His people in the early church. We have the opportunity to use our tables as places of reconciliation, forgiveness, grace, and generosity. Our tables can serve as level fields where our preconceptions are laid aside and we can see the face of Jesus in every guest. When we draw people together at our tables, let us do it in the same spirit as Christ. In eating together, let us remember the body that was given to bless us. And in drinking, let us join together in the unity of Jesus, who, through His self-giving love for us, makes all things new.

Table Talk

CONVERSATION STARTERS

1. If Jesus intended His followers to be "united in heart and mind," why do you think we are so often divided? Describe some of the discord and division you have witnessed in churches or Christian groups.

2. Describe a time when you really felt a sense of unity among your brothers and sisters in Christ. What was it like? What do you think inspired it?

3. Different churches and Christian groups celebrate Communion (Eucharist, the Lord's Supper) differently. What practices in your own fellowship are particularly meaningful to you? Why?

4. What prejudices or fears tend to separate you from other people, especially other Christians? What are some ways to minimize those prejudices or fears?

DIGGING DEEPER

1. *"Since God chose you to be the holy people he loves, you must clothe yourselves with tenderhearted mercy, kindness, humility, gentleness, and patience. Make allowance for each other's faults, and forgive anyone who offends you. Remember, the Lord forgave you, so you must forgive others. Above all, clothe yourselves with love, which binds us all together in perfect harmony"* (COLOSSIANS 3:12-14).

   a. The values we choose are the way we "dress" when we interact with others; they show our proper image to the world. List three characteristics you want to "wear" when you meet others today. Pray that God will help you dress yourself in the fruits of His good and grace-giving Spirit, so that you will be prepared to pass that grace along to others.

   b. Just as the proper undergarments determine the fit and appearance of an outfit, our inner attitudes determine how we "wear" our values. According to this verse, what is the fundamental experience and attitude that makes everything else work? How does this one "garment" affect all the others?

2. *"There are different kinds of spiritual gifts, but the same Spirit is the source of them all. There are different kinds of service, but we serve the same Lord. God works in different ways, but it is the same God who does the work in all of us"* (1 CORINTHIANS 12:4-6).

   a. When we serve our fellow believers, we are really serving the presence of Christ in them. When we don't use our gifts in service to others in the body of Christ, in a sense we are turning away from Jesus. List at least two specific ways you are using—or could use—your spiritual gifts to honor Jesus, serve your fellow Christians, and build unity in the body of Christ. Then list two ways you can use your gifts to serve those outside the community of faith.

   b. Do you sometimes find yourself in conflict with others because of your differences? Remember that in Christ, though we are unified, we each play a different part in God's dynamic Kingdom. Think of someone you know who seems particularly different from you. How do those differences affect the way you interact? Write down a gift that you see in that person. Pray that God will grow that gift in his or her life and will help you focus on that person's strengths rather than the frustrations that arise from differences.

3. *"This is real love—not that we loved God, but that he loved us and sent his Son as a sacrifice to take away our sins. Dear friends, since God loved us that much, we surely ought to love each other. No one has ever seen God. But if we love one another, God lives in us, and his love is brought to full expression in us"* (1 JOHN 4:10-12).

   a. According to this verse, what enables us to truly love others?

   b. John says that no one has ever seen God. But when we allow the love of God in our lives to overflow into others' lives, somehow the face of Jesus comes shining through. In what ways have you been gifted to see Jesus in others? In what ways do you think (or hope) they see Jesus in you?

c. Not everyone is easy to love. But when we hold other Christians' weaknesses against them instead of looking at them through the lens of God's everlasting love, Jesus becomes more difficult for us to see and comprehend. It is only when we lay down our grievances at the feet of Jesus that we are able to truly know Him, to see Him present in the people around us and in our lives. Think of a person you find especially difficult to love. Make a list of the things that frustrate you most about that person. Then really stretch your mind and write a description of that person as you imagine God sees him or her. Pray over both lists, asking for a heart of love, forgiveness, and unity with both God and others.

Notes

1. [Thomas Cranmer,] "Proper 28 (The Sunday Closest to November 16)," *The Book of Common Prayer* (New York: Church Publishing, 1979), 236.
2. C. S. Lewis, "What the Bird Said Early in the Year," quoted on the memorial plaque at Addison's Walk, Magdalen College, Oxford University, at C. S. Lewis Institute: Discipleship of Heart and Mind (website), http://www.cslewisinstitute.org/photos/image/834#image-load.
3. Victor Hugo, *Les Misérables*, tr. Isabel F. Hapgood (New York: Thomas Y. Crowell, 1887), 73, accessed as a Google book at https://books.google.com/books?id=XdwPAAAAYAAJ&printsec=frontcover&source=gbs_ge_summary_r&cad=0#v=onepage&q&f=false.

About the Authors

Sally Clarkson is the mother of four wholehearted children, a popular conference speaker, and a champion of women everywhere. Since founding Whole Heart Ministries with her husband, Clay, Sally has inspired thousands of women through her blog and podcasts. She is the bestselling author of numerous books and articles on Christian motherhood and parenting, including *The Lifegiving Home* (with Sarah Clarkson), *Own Your Life*, *Desperate* (with Sarah Mae), *The Mission of Motherhood*, *The Ministry of Motherhood*, and most recently, *Different: The Story of an Outside-the-Box Kid and the Mom Who Loved Him* (with Nathan Clarkson).

Sally lives in Monument, Colorado, and loves Jesus, her family, reading, music, tea, traveling, long walks, and her golden retriever, Darcy.

Her passion is to mentor women and to disciple them to become the women they were created to be.

Joel Clarkson is an award-winning composer who is known for the vibrant colors of sound he paints with his music. Joel has provided original award-winning music for numerous feature and short films, and his creative contributions to concert music as a composer and orchestrator have been heard around the world to great acclaim. His love for producing creative content led him into Christian publishing, where he has coauthored two books, *The Lifegiving Home Experience* and *A Different Kind of Hero* (both with Tyndale Momentum), and into audiobook narration, where his work on the beloved children's fantasy *The Green Ember* was nominated in Audible's "Best of 2015" Editor's Picks in the children's category. For more information, please visit www.joelclarkson.com.

Joy Clarkson is a lover of God and people, a crafter of words, and a dedicated evangelist for Yorkshire Gold Tea. Joy studied Rhetorical Communications at Biola University, and is currently a postgraduate student in Theology, Imagination, and the Arts at the University of St. Andrews in Scotland, where she enjoys long walks on the shore of the North Sea and obscure Scottish fairy tales. Joy fills her days with academic research, music making, adventuring, and savoring deep conversations with her soul friends.

MAKE YOUR TABLE
a delightful, lifegiving space where your family and friends long to be.

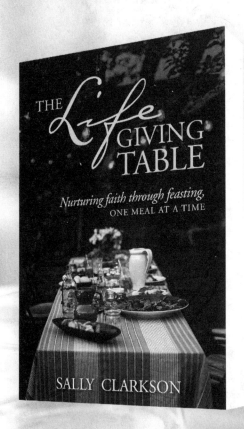

In *The Lifegiving Table,* Sally shares stories about her own family's table talk and faith-shaped conversations, as well as favorite recipes and practical ideas to draw you closer to the people you love.

WWW.TYNDALE.COM

THE *Life* GIVING SERIES

BY SALLY CLARKSON

Learn how to make your home the place
your friends and family long to be.

CP1307